Images of Jesus Today

Fay Oliver

Images of Jesus Today

Edited by
James H. Charlesworth
and Walter P. Weaver

Faith and Scholarship Colloquies 3
Florida Southern College

Trinity Press International   Valley Forge, Pa.

First Published 1994

Trinity Press International
P.O. Box 851
Valley Forge, PA 19482–0851

Copyright © 1994 Trinity Press International

Cover Design by Brian Preuss

Library of Congress Cataloging-in-Publication Data

Images of Jesus today / edited by James H. Charlesworth and Walter P. Weaver.
 p. cm. — (Faith and scholarship colloquies ; 3)
 Includes bibliographical references and index.
 ISBN 1-56338-082-X
 1. Jesus Christ—Person and offices. 2. Jesus Christ—Historicity. 3. Jesus Christ—History of doctrines—20th century.
 I. Charlesworth, James H. II. Weaver, Walter P. III. Series.
 BT205.I5 1994
 232–dc20   94-993
                                                       CIP

Printed in the United States of America

94 95 96 97 98 99   10 9 8 7 6 5 4 3 2 1

To
our friend and colleague
JOHN W. COOK
celebrating
his warm spirit
and
caring friendship

Contents

Contributors

JAMES H. CHARLESWORTH is the George W. Collord Professor of New Testament Language and Literature at Princeton Theological Seminary.

MARCUS J. BORG is Hundere Distinguished Professor of Religion and Culture at Oregon State University.

RICHARD A. HORSLEY is Professor and Chair, Study of Religion Program, the University of Massachusetts at Boston.

DORON MENDELS is Professor and Chair, Department of History, the Hebrew University of Jerusalem.

WALTER P. WEAVER is Chair of the Humanities Division and the Department of Religion and Philosophy and holds the Pendergrass Chair in Religion at Florida Southern College.

Faith and Scholarship Colloquies

This series explores the boundaries where faith and academic study intersect. At these borders, the sharp edge of current biblical scholarship is allowed to cut theologically and pose its often challenging questions for traditional faith. The series includes contributions from leading scholars in contemporary biblical studies. As Christian faith seeks to send a word on target in our day, as powerful as those in the past, it needs to sharpen its perception and proclamation from honest and truthful insights in human knowledge, from first-century archaeology to modern linguistics.

Foreword

Reflections on the Continuing Quest for Jesus

The historical Jesus continues to fascinate — not only Christians, but also Jews, both in America and throughout the world. Twenty-five years ago there was hardly a stir in the house of Jesus studies; the views of the dominant figure of the time, Rudolf Bultmann, had spread the gospel of silence — historical and theological — over the terrain occupied by the question of the historical Jesus. And even though something called (somewhat pretentiously) the "new quest" of the historical Jesus was lurking about in the historical quest for Jesus, it failed to summon any substantial effort and finally revealed itself as largely a puttering around in Bultmann's garden. Its grandest bequest was the evolution of redaction criticism, which exposed and clarified the theologies of each evangelist; but its assumptions remained mostly confined to Bultmann's insights, i.e., existentialist interpretation based on stringent form-critical analysis.[1]

The landscape looks significantly different today. A new outburst of works on the historical Jesus has appeared, stimulated by new methods, more comprehensive literary sources, and more extensive archaeological evidence from Jesus' time. Whether there is also some kind of theological force arising to drive this new interest in the historical Jesus remains yet to come clear; at this stage what seems more characteristic of this new movement is a lack of any special interest in the theological significance of its subject. Of course, historians are entitled to investigate whatever subject arouses their passions, but most of the investigators appear to belong to some kind of religious tradition (or bias) as well. Bultmann claimed that his interest in the historical Jesus was that of the historian seeking different self-understandings, i.e., an encounter with a historical figure poses a challenge to my own understanding of existence that might offer me an alternative.[2] Surely that remains a possible motive for investigating the past, though I also seem to recall just how kerygmatic Bultmann's picture of the historical Jesus sounded, with that insistent call for decision about the (existential) proclamation of the Kingdom. The following from Bultmann is typical:

> In this last hour, the hour of decision, Jesus is sent with the final, decisive word. Happy is he who understands it and is not offended in him! (Matt. 11:6) Decision is inevitable... for him or against him: "He who is not with me is against me, and he who does not gather with me scatters" (Matt. 12:30).
> ... the kingdom of God is deliverance for men. It is that *eschatological* deliverance which ends everything earthly. This deliverance is the only deliverance which can properly be so called; therefore it demands of man decision. It is not something which man can possess along with other good things, which he may pursue along with other interests. This deliverance confronts man as an Either-Or.[3]

However Kierkegaardian that *Entweder-Oder* must have sounded, the sense of urgency and the ultimacy of the decision evoke the kerygmatic tone, though, of course, Bultmann denied that his book on Jesus was in any sense kerygma.[4]

Nevertheless, one of the unresolved matters, in fact

still left over from the "old quest" of the historical Jesus, pertains to the theological weight or import posed by the whole question of the significance of the historical Jesus for faith. Not much attention is at present devoted to this issue, though here and there one can detect some concern with it. One of the marks of Bultmann's greatness was that he at least raised the giant theological questions and posed an answer to them. His answer to the question of the historical Jesus was certainly brilliant and shaped the response of a whole generation. He (perhaps along with Barth) taught us to think that faith was essentially independent of historical investigation, that faith required nothing more than some acknowledgment of Jesus' existence (with the crucifixion somehow included) — the famous *Dass* or "thatness" of Jesus' historical factuality. Bultmann (or so certainly he thought) was leaning on Paul, not to mention John and, with reference to later times, Luther.[5] This somewhat constricted response, which seemed to negate any theological significance to the whole enterprise of inquiry into the historical Jesus, gave rise to the "new quest" with its question about the continuity between Jesus' proclamation and the early church's claims about Jesus as the resurrected Christ and Lord. But the question was formulated in strictly Bultmannian terms and never really seemed to advance much beyond those presuppositions.[6] The matter then still remains open: What is the importance, if any, for the Christian faith today of the whole issue that passes under the heading of "historical Jesus"? Some of the essays in this volume, while not necessarily directing themselves primarily to this question, nevertheless involve it and suggest some ways of approaching it.

There also remain unresolved questions pertaining to the historical problem of investigating the "life" of Jesus in the first instance. Surely among these is the issue of methodology. Form criticism — or perhaps better now something like tradition history — still remains a presupposition in dealing with the literary texts, although its criteria have been appropriately modified. The exclusion

of Jesus traditions not related either to Judaism or to the
early church is almost universally rejected as a far too rigid
principle; this principle of discontinuity leads to a picture
of a Jesus who was not a Jew and to a Christianity dissociated from Jesus. Ultimately, Jesus is marked out only as
"unique."

Especially the recovery of a Jesus in his Judaic environment is characteristic of the newer research. The careful
elucidation of that environment, and indeed the cross-
cultural examination of the Hellenistic-Jewish world of
ancient Palestine in which Jesus moved, has been enor-
mously fruitful in recent years.[7] In addition, sociological
studies along with better textual approaches have opened
up new possibilities in understanding Jesus and his world.
But agreement on procedure, appropriate texts, and general conclusions remains somewhat elusive. A sophisticated thinking-through of these methodological issues can
be found in the works of John Dominic Crossan and John
Meier.[8] The healthy discussion of their arguments has
already begun. Whether one finds their specific results
compelling or not, it is clear that their methodological de-
cisions must be included in future Jesus Research. Other
approaches are documented in impressive thoroughness in
the initial essay of this volume by James H. Charlesworth.

Connected with the methodological question is the
matter of terminological confusion. Certain categories or
labels have been used for a long time in the studies of
biblical scholars, but there seems to be hardly any consistency in their use. For example, there are those who
would characterize the message of Jesus as "apocalyptic,"[9]
while others would wish to say that it was "eschatological," though not "apocalyptic," and there is a substantial
movement now that would deny to Jesus any kind of eschatological proclamation. The last is represented in this
volume in the essay by Marcus Borg, who is, however,
careful to describe just how he wishes to use the terms "eschatology," "eschatological," and "apocalyptic" as applied
to the message of the historical Jesus.[10] Not everyone is so

careful, however, and there remains a kind of semantic bog with respect to the ways scholars have been using these terms.

A similar confusion seems to prevail regarding the expression used above that is associated with Bultmann: self-understanding. Bultmann, following the school of Heidegger and, prior to that, Wilhelm Dilthey, used the expression to denote an understanding of existence. Such an understanding might or might not be consciously articulated, which is of no importance to the historical investigator; more likely a self-understanding (an understanding of the self as constituted in the world) is disclosed in one's deeds and words. Bultmann was careful to distinguish this self-understanding (*Selbstverständnis*) from self-consciousness (*Selbstbewusstsein*), which he regarded as a psychological category and inappropriate to apply to the historical Jesus, since the knowledge of Jesus' psyche is inaccessible to us, i.e., what Jesus may have thought of himself Bultmann regarded as unknowable. (That would also imply that whether Jesus actualized his own self-understanding in an act of self-consciousness is likewise unknowable.) In research works today, however, the term "self-understanding" seems to appear as virtually indistinguishable from self-consciousness, or at least in reference to how Jesus must have thought about himself.[11] Such semantic usage doubtless causes some uneasy whirring of the Bultmannian spirits, and for the advancement of common discourse perhaps everyone using the terminology should be expected to say what he or she means by it at the outset.

Other specific questions hang around to disturb studies of the historical Jesus. For example, not unimportant to anyone asking about Jesus' statements regarding his own role or mission is the question of the Son of Man tradition. Did Jesus speak of the Son of Man, in particular of an eschatological Son of Man, and did he refer to himself in this way? It is possible still to find any and every answer to this question, e.g., Yes and No in both ways, and Who knows?

As long as there exists no consensus on this one question alone, the study of Jesus, and especially his apparent representation of his own activity, will remain veiled (certainly in part), and, in any case, the answer that anyone gives to it will necessarily shape the overall picture of Jesus that emerges. Some of the possibilities can be seen in the essays by James H. Charlesworth and Marcus J. Borg in this volume.

And there is the matter, finally, with which we all are familiar enough from the influence of Schweitzer's classic study[12] on the problem of the historical Jesus, i.e., the sometimes wildly varying pictures that have come forth from "objective" historical readings of the evidence. The very title of this present volume of essays points to the problem and is intended, in part, to demonstrate it. Among the more recent possibilities is the reading of Jesus that sees him as a Cynic or Cynic-like figure, and the movement that he started as evolving from Cynic influences. Richard A. Horsley examines this hypothesis in his essay and discloses its essential problematic. Similarly, Doron Mendels looks at the possibility, enjoying some currency again after these many years, that Jesus was much more profoundly involved in the political struggles of his time than has traditionally been allowed.[13] These varying images of Jesus, born out of a claimed historical *Wissenschaft*, point not only to the unfinished nature of all historical work, but perhaps also to the curious, tenacious power of the Jesus paradigm to continue to tantalize and haunt the imagination of every age.

I invite the reader to engage the questions raised in the following pages, to struggle with these significant issues, and hopefully to deepen an understanding of the available answers and the veritable sea change that has occurred in pursuit of that profoundly vexatious but mesmerizing enterprise known broadly as Jesus Research.[14]

Certain persons need to be acknowledged for their contributions to this volume. In addition to the essayists, the secretary of the Department of Religion and Philosophy at Florida Southern College, Beverly Johnson, deserves our gratitude for perseverance in preparation of manuscripts; and the president of the college, Robert A. Davis, merits our special thanks for continuing support of the symposia at Florida Southern College that form the basis for this work (and is embodied in the logo of this series). And a particular word of thanks goes to Dr. Harold Rast, the editorial director of Trinity Press International, for his continuing interest in and support of the works deriving from these symposia.

Walter P. Weaver

NOTES

1. "Existentialist interpretation" refers to Bultmann's practice of interpreting the various messages of the New Testament in the categories of existence provided by the philosophy of Martin Heidegger. Form criticism, as is generally known, was pioneered by Bultmann (and Martin Dibelius) and describes the categorization of oral tradition into recognizable "forms" and consequent passing of a judgment on their historicity. It is particularly applicable to the process of reconstructing the message of Jesus out of the synoptic material.

2. See, e.g., his statement in Hans Barstch, ed., *Kerygma and Myth: A Theological Debate*, trans. Reginald H. Fuller (New York: Harper, 1961), 117.

3. *Jesus and the Word*, trans. Louise Pettibone Smith and Erminie Huntress Lantero (New York: Charles Scribner's Sons, 1934), 30, 35.

4. See note 2 above.

5. It is, of course, not the case that Luther had any knowledge about what we today call the "historical Jesus," but Bultmann certainly regarded the claim of securing the immunity of faith from the vagaries of historical research as an extension of the principle of justification on the basis of faith.

6. One can see in a work like Günther Bornkamm's *Jesus of Nazareth* (trans. Irene and Fraser McLuskey with James M. Robinson [New York: Harper, 1960]), where the major differences from Bultmann lay, and they had mostly to do with matters of emphasis, e.g., seeing the connectedness of kerygma and message of Jesus wherever possible.

7. E.g., see the references in the essay by James H. Charlesworth in this volume.

8. Crossan in *The Historical Jesus: The Life of a Mediterranean Jewish Peasant* (San Francisco: Harper San Francisco, 1992); and Meier in *A Marginal Jew: Rethinking the Historical Jesus,* Anchor Bible Reference Library (New York: Doubleday, 1991). Meier's discussion of the sources and criteria for determining authenticity is judicious, thorough, and balanced. Crossan's approach combines cross-cultural and anthropological analysis, along with a stratigraphical layering of the texts that elevates the criterion of multiple attestation to the center. A number of less obvious moves occurs along the way, such as judgments on the value of apocryphal literature (Thomas, etc.), which remain controversial. The resulting picture of Jesus is, however, extremely interesting, to say the least. Meier's work remains unfinished at this point, and a second volume is expected.

9. One of the expected volumes in this series takes up the question of apocalypticism and apocalyptic eschatology.

10. The reader will note from the Borg essay that it is imminent expectation of the end of the world that Borg wishes to deny to the historical Jesus, and it is for that position that he uses the term "imminent eschatology." The confusion in the discussion can be seen in the fact that, for example, Ernst Käsemann used virtually the same definition for the word "apocalyptic." See Käsemann's essay in *New Testament Questions of Today,* trans. W. J. Montague (Philadelphia: Fortress, 1969), 109, n. 1, where apocalyptic is described as expectation of "imminent parousia."

11. See the effort to make a careful distinction in these terms in James H. Charlesworth, *Jesus within Judaism: New Light from Exciting Archaeological Discoveries,* Anchor Bible Reference Library (New York: Doubleday, 1988), 131–36 and ensuing examples. Charlesworth is willing to talk about a *messianic* self-understanding, i.e., a "messianic" interpretation of existence that Jesus presumably applied to himself. For useful reflections on the Bultmannian use of "self-understanding," see John MacQuarrie, *The Scope of Demythologizing: Bultmann and His Critics* (New York: Harper, 1960), especially 232ff, and also in MacQuarrie's earlier work, *An Existentialist Theology: A Comparison of Heidegger and Bultmann* (New York and Evanston: Harper, 1965; originally published by SCM Press, 1955), especially 65–66, 199–204. MacQuarrie makes it clear that for Bultmann, as for Heidegger, the concept of a self-understanding arose out of the analysis of *Dasein's* being-in-the world as a characteristic of

understanding generally. Bultmann took over the analysis and applied it to the New Testament and in particular characterized the impact of the kerygma, when received in faith, as producing a new self-understanding in which the claims of the self are surrendered and existence is construed as based entirely on grace.

12. *The Quest of the Historical Jesus*, trans. W. Montgomery (London: Adam and Charles Black, 1910), since reissued many times.

13. See also his recent work, *The Rise and Fall of Jewish Nationalism: Jewish and Christian Ethnicity in Ancient Palestine*, Anchor Bible Reference Library (New York: Doubleday, 1992).

14. A good survey of the recent literature is that of Craig A. Evans, *Jesus*, IBR Bibliographies No. 5 (Grand Rapids: Baker Book House, 1992). It is an updated and abridged version of the author's more expansive and scholarly *Life of Jesus Research: An Annotated Bibliography*, New Testament Tools and Studies 13 (Leiden: Brill, 1989).

Chapter 1

Jesus Research Expands with Chaotic Creativity

James H. Charlesworth

INTRODUCTION

Since the mid-1960s my research has focused on the Old Testament Pseudepigrapha;[1] hence, my reflections on Jesus Research sometimes resonate with potent images remembered from reading one of the Pseudepigrapha. In wrestling with the scope and variety of contemporary Jesus Research, I am reminded of the metaphor of shepherds in the Books of Enoch. In one of the earliest Jewish apocalypses Enoch sees the leaders of Israel acting as shepherds. The guidance given by them causes confusion and chaos. In the Dream Visions Enoch reports, "Again I saw those sheep, how they went astray, going in diverse ways and abandoning that house of his" (1 Enoch 89:51). To some observers, scholars pursuing Jesus Research may seem like shepherds who have led sheep in diverse ways. Is there a consensus today among the best scholars engaged in Jesus Research or is there chaotic creativity?

In the late 1960s Hugh Anderson, noting that over

sixty thousand so-called biographies of Jesus had been
published, asked, "Who of sufficient range of intellect and
breadth of vision is to survey and measure an enterprise so
massive, to bring some order into the chaos of the Lives of
Jesus?"[2] The task before us now is formidable, and in some
ways impossible. I can only attempt to present what seems
to be going on from my own vantage point and to try to
represent a balanced judgment.

Mutually exclusive models are now being proposed
for reconstructing the life of Jesus of Nazareth. Is Jesus
to be seen as a Cynic philosopher, as Burton L. Mack
claims,[3] or a Jewish prophet, as David Aune, David Hill,
and so many other scholars have concluded?[4] Was he influenced by apocalypticism, as E. P. Sanders, Christopher
Rowland, J. D. G. Dunn, and many other scholars argue,[5]
or was he essentially noneschatological, as Marcus J. Borg
has claimed recently?[6] Are we to withdraw into literary
criticism and be content with seeking to understand the
theologies of the evangelists or should we enrich Jesus
Research with insights garnered from sociology?

Did Jesus exist? This is the most obvious question with
which to begin. It is not a new concern. One hundred and
forty years ago Bruno Bauer and sixty years ago P.-L. Couchoud advanced the conclusion that Jesus never existed.[7]
They claimed the reference to Jesus by Josephus was added
by a Christian and that the evangelists were creating out
of Old Testament prophecies not only a life of Jesus but
his historical existence. Recently a professor of German at
Birkbeck College, University of London, G. A. Wells, concludes in *The Historical Evidence for Jesus* and more recently
in *Who Was Jesus?* that the reason scholars are perplexed
by the search for the historical Jesus is because he never
existed.[8] Wells is no amateur, and he has studied the sec-
ondary literature carefully, citing such eminent authorities
as Raymond E. Brown, Dwight Moody Smith, C. H. Dodd,
Hans Conzelmann, Joseph Fitzmyer, K. Barrett, and J. D. G.
Dunn. He is very impressed that Paul never seems interested in the pre-Easter Jesus. Persuaded by the passages in

the Gospels that are clearly additions to earlier Jesus traditions, he concludes that the evangelists and others created
the historicity of Jesus.

He fails to observe that the evangelists inherited earlier
traditions, and that some of these are certainly very early,
and even pre-Easter. He does comprehend that the evangelists were indeed editors, adding to traditions; but he fails
to grasp that as *editors* they were receiving traditions to ex-
pand and that most of these were not directly from the Old
Testament. He does not adequately note the offensive nature of the Gospel accounts that cannot be attributed to the
evangelists. These passages embarrassing to them, and not
added by Jesus' followers, would include the failure of the
disciples to understand Jesus' teachings, Jesus' rebuke that
Peter was acting like Satan, James's and John's request to
sit on thrones, Judas's inclusion as one of the twelve and
his betrayal of Jesus, Peter's denials, the rejection of Jesus
by his family, and Jesus' crucifixion. All these traditions
were inherited by the evangelists, and every one of them
antedates Jesus' death in 30 C.E.

Wells correctly observes that the historical reconstruction of Jesus and his time must be according to the highest
historiography; hence he rejects the confessional approach
of many Christians and the distortions of the evidence
caused by some Christian theologians. He, however, does
not seem to recognize the faith-centered approach in his
own work. Note these words of faith in his own position: "I do not myself *believe* that the earliest (pre-Gospel)
Christian literature supports" the conclusion that Jesus
was crucified around 30 C.E., and that those who "became
convinced of his Resurrection" included some who "had
known him before his death."[9] Wells is led to conclude that
there are good reasons to doubt that Jesus ever existed.[10]

In a book that appeared about the same time as Wells's
Who Was Jesus? and bearing the same title, Hendrikus
Boers of Emory University presents a penetrating and rig-
orous examination of the Jesus traditions. He has become
aware of how much the impressions left by Jesus have

affected the narratives about him. But, far from conclud-
ing that such accounts are therefore unhistorical, he points
out that this adulation results from the power of Jesus himself. Boers even goes on to conclude that Jesus "may have
been involved in armed resistance against Rome."[11] These
works bearing the same title are a powerful indication of
the breadth of possibilities in Jesus Research.

The publications dedicated to Jesus Research have increased markedly over the last two decades. The extent of
that research is reflected in P. M. Beaude's *Jésus de Nazareth*,[12] Herbert Leroy's *Jesus: Überlieferung und Deutung*,[13]
and especially in two major publications. In *The Lives of
Jesus* Warren S. Kissinger attempts to present a representative bibliography of lives of Jesus until the early 1980s.[14]
Even more important for an assessment of Jesus Research
today is Craig A. Evans's *Life of Jesus Research: An Annotated
Bibliography*, which was published by Brill in 1989,[15] and
John Reumann's review of Jesus Research in the Society of
Biblical Literature's centennial publication on New Testa-
ment study.[16] In *Jesus' Jewishness*, which appeared in 1991,
the Roman Catholic New Testament scholar John P. Meier
presented his scholarly reflections on the present state of
Jesus Research; he expanded these reflections in his recent
A Marginal Jew.[17]

International experts in Jesus Research employ the
same method. They observe and acknowledge the evangelists' theological tendencies, then seek to discern behind
them traditions inherited by the evangelists, and finally to
judge which of these seem to derive with some reliable
probability from Jesus. The criterion of discontinuity —
that is, what is not attributable to Judaism or Jesus' followers may in fact be attributable to him — is rapidly falling
out of fashion. As many scholars have stressed, attempts to
distance Jesus from Judaism in order to elevate his uniqueness are hardly acceptable as scientific research. Today
scholars wisely emphasize that we must employ numerous methods, including form criticism, redaction criticism,
literary criticism, sociology, archaeology, and even other

methods. By employing more than one method it is possible to check and improve the results obtained by others.

CONSENSUS

Are scholars involved in Jesus Research like the leaders in Enoch's vision who are "shepherds and their colleagues" that have "handed over those sheep to all the wild beasts so that they might devour them" (1 Enoch 89:68)? I do not think this picture is an adequate assessment of the present state of research. Let me briefly point to twenty areas of consensus among experts involved in Jesus Research.

First, it is widely acknowledged that Jesus was a Jew. In fact only one influential author has denied this fact: H. Stewart Chamberlain.[18] Jesus' Jewishness was assumed and his obedience to Torah and Temple were demonstrated most notably by David Flusser (in *Jesus* and in *Judaism and the Origins of Christianity*),[19] Ed Sanders (in *Jesus and Judaism* and in *Jewish Law from Jesus to the Mishnah*)[20] and myself (in *Jesus within Judaism*, in *Jesus' Jewishness*, and in *Jesus and the Dead Sea Scrolls*).

Second, it is widely acknowledged today that it is not possible to write a biography of Jesus; yet his earliest followers had some interest in Jesus' life and teachings. Otherwise one could not explain the appearance of the Gospels after 60 C.E. As the Scot James S. Stewart stated, the Gospels are a "set of memoirs," a selection of "historical reminiscences."[21] The best summary of what can be reported regarding the historical Jesus may still be Günther Bornkamm's *Jesus of Nazareth*.[22] Bornkamm was one of Bultmann's most prominent students, but he broke with his teacher's insistence that knowledge of Jesus' life was not only impossible but also irrelevant for Christian faith.

Third, today in contrast to twenty years ago, many scholars acknowledge that we do possess considerable knowledge about the historical Jesus. Note, for example, Sanders's claim: "The dominant view today seems to be that we can know pretty well what Jesus was out to accomplish, that we can know a lot about what he said, and that those two things make sense within the world of first-century Judaism."[23]

Contemporary scholars simply no longer accept the pessimism of the great New Testament expert Rudolf Bultmann, who claimed that Jesus was a presupposition of New Testament theology[24] and in *Jesus and the Word* concluded as follows:

> I do indeed think that we can know almost nothing concerning the life and personality of Jesus, since the early Christian sources show no interest in either, are moreover fragmentary and often legendary; and other sources about Jesus do not exist.[25]

This extreme position was somewhat later modified by Bultmann himself,[26] and it does not seem representative of much of his own work. While Bultmann stressed that knowledge of Jesus' "life and personality" was not essential to confess his Lordship and that Jesus' message can only be a presupposition of Christian theology, because it was not "Christian," he did affirm that it is "overwhelmingly" probable that "Jesus is the bearer of the message,"[27] that the existence of Jesus and his crucifixion is a necessity for faith, and that the historian can supply far more reliable information regarding the historical Jesus than the believer needs to comprehend. These points are now clarified by the Australian New Testament scholar John Painter.[28] Certainly Bultmann's position has been more caricatured than understood; it is wise to remember that the highest probability in historical reconstructions does not establish or elicit the faith contained in the earliest confessions (kerygmata).

Today, in contrast to Bultmann's time, it is now being recognized that there is considerable and reliable bedrock historical material in the Gospels. For example, in the 1960s David Flusser launched his book on Jesus with these words:

The main purpose of this book is to show that it is possible to write the story of Jesus.... With the exception of the historian Flavius Josephus, and possibly St. Paul, among the Jews of post–Old Testament times Jesus is the one about whom we know most.[29]

Similarly, William R. Farmer in 1982 claimed that we "have access to a large body of first-rate historical evidence that is decisive in answering important questions about Jesus."[30]

American specialists like David E. Aune, John P. Meier, James M. Robinson, and E. P. Sanders, Scottish New Testament experts like Hugh Anderson and J. C. O'Neill, Israeli historians like David Flusser, Doron Mendels, and Daniel R. Schwartz, German professors like Ernst Käsemann,[31] Martin Hengel, Hermann Lichtenberger, and Johann Maier, English scholars like G. N. Stanton and Geza Vermes, French and Swiss New Testament experts like Pierre Benoit and E. Trocmé, Scandinavian specialists like Peder Borgen, Nils Dahl, and Harald Riesenfeld, Dutch scholars like Edward Schillebeeckx and Marinus de Jonge, Australian specialists like John Painter and Max Wilcox, Italian experts like Paolo Sacchi and Cardinal Martini — in fact far too many international authorities to mention — are all, and independently, recognizing that in its broad outline the Gospels' account of Jesus is substantially reliable and true.[32] In summary, this is the conclusion of the perceptive former archbishop of Canterbury, J. Ramsey,[33] the Oxford scholar A. E. Harvey,[34] the former bishop of the Church of Sweden Gustaf Aulén,[35] the present holder of the Lightfoot chair in Durham, England, J. D. G. Dunn,[36] and the Duke scholar Sanders. Along with the best Jewish scholars pursuing Jesus Research, notably Flusser, Rivkin, and Vermes, ultraconservative and ultraliberal Christian scholars have reached this same conclusion. Even liberation theologians, like Juan Luis Segundo in his *The Historical Jesus of the Synoptics*,[37] are stressing the importance of the historical Jesus.

Fourth, scholars are now trying to comprehend *Jesus in his time and within the Judaism he knew.* This endeavor is found in the publications of Borg, Chilton, Dunn, Harvey, Hengel, Horsley, Meier, Meyer, Mendels, Riches, Sanders, Theissen, and many other experts.[38] As Leander Keck, the former dean of Yale Divinity School, concludes, Jesus must be studied not only in light of the church but also in light of Early Judaism, that is "not only from what he produced but from what produced him."[39]

Fifth, many scholars have come to conclude that Jesus led some kind of renewal movement. This insight, with impressive variations, is shared by Sanders and Horsley. In writing *Jesus within Judaism* I was surprised to come to the conclusion that the concept of twelve disciples was not created by Jesus' followers.[40] Judas is always in the list of twelve; hence the idea of a special group of twelve must antedate the crucifixion in 30 C.E.. Later I was startled to observe that Sanders in *Jesus in Judaism* had arrived at the same conclusion.[41] Sanders and I take this clearly symbolic action to denote Jesus' attempt to restore Israel. As Gerhard Lohfink stresses in *Jesus and Community*, creating a group of twelve disciples "exemplified the awakening of Israel and its gathering in the eschatological salvific community."[42]

Sixth, many critics have now concluded that Jesus' attack against the money-changers in the Temple probably was the major stimulus to his condemnation and death.[43] This conclusion is typical of Sanders.[44] Borg, who differs from Sanders radically, also sees Jesus' opposition to the Temple as a major factor, but for him the Temple cult is rejected by Jesus because of its concept of holiness as separation.[45]

Seventh, Galilee has become a major focus of study. Sean Freyne has published numerous studies on Jesus and his Galilean background; the latest volume appeared in 1988 and is titled *Galilee, Jesus and the Gospels.*[46] In 1989 Sherman E. Johnson published *Jesus and His Towns*[47] which is an attractive, popular book that would have been much improved if it had incorporated the new insights obtained by the Israeli and American archaeologists working in Galilee. The importance of Galilee in Jesus Research appears in a book edited by Lee I. Levine and titled *The Galilee in Late Antiquity.*[48] A popular, richly illustrated book, based on superb topographical sensitivity and a synthetic conservative approach to archaeological discoveries pertaining to Jesus is B. Pixner's *With Jesus through Galilee according to the Fifth Gospel* (the fifth gospel is topographa or "a Geography of Salvation").[49]

The motive for Judas's betrayal may no longer be so mysterious. If Iscariot means *ish karioth*, then he was from Karioth, which is probably in southern Judaea. Hence, Judas would be the only non-Galilean among Jesus' disciples. Did he have a Judaean interpretation of the Messiah as one who would drive the Romans out of Jerusalem, precisely as the Judaean Psalms of Solomon indicated?[50] Judas is an enigmatic figure and the transmission of traditions concerning him was clearly not motivated by a desire to be historically accurate.[51]

Eighth, Jesus is now recognized to have been a devout Jew. He went to Jerusalem on the Passover pilgrimage and revered the Temple, recognizing it as the House in which to pray.[52] Flusser has suggested that Jesus should be considered a hasid, that is, one who elevated the concept of Torah and increased its demands.[53] Sanders clearly shows that Jesus obeyed the Torah.[54]

Ninth, the past twenty years have seen an incredible increase in primary sources from Jesus' time. Work is progressing throughout the world in the attempt to ascertain how and in what ways the Jewish writings help us understand the historical Jesus. Most important among these writings are the Old Testament Pseudepigrapha and the Dead Sea Scrolls. Scholars focused on this fruitful area include Flusser in Israel, Braun and Hengel in Germany, Dunn in England, and Kee in the United States. Helpful works are Herbert Braun's *Jesus: Der Mann aus Nazareth und seine Zeit*[55] and my own *Jesus within Judaism.*[56] Leading experts have contributed major studies on the relation of Jesus to the apocryphal writings and the Dead Sea Scrolls in two volumes, titled *Jesus' Jewishness* and *Jesus and the Dead Sea Scrolls*.[57]

Tenth, while the Jewish writings contemporaneous with Jesus are stimulating exciting new possibilities, it is wise to remember that Jesus never quoted from any of them. He did, however, frequently quote from the collection of scrolls called the "Old Testament." It is widely recognized that Jesus' proclamations were based on the accepted authority of these biblical books.

Eleventh, most experts on Jesus and the Judaism of his day have concurred that he was significantly influenced by apocalyptic thought and that his message was eschatological. This prevailing position has been dominant since Weiss's *Die Predigt Jesu vom Reiche Gottes*, which appeared in 1892.[58] That Jesus was shaped by Jewish apocalypticism has undergirded such magisterial works as Albert Schweitzer's *Vom Reimarus zu Wrede*,[59] Norman Perrin's *The Kingdom of God*,[60] and Howard Clark Kee's *Jesus in History*.[61] One of the strongest consensuses in New Testament research is that Jesus' mission was to proclaim the dawning of God's Rule, the Kingdom of God. Research on Mark 9:1 has convinced virtually every specialist that Jesus' teaching was emphatically apocalyptic and eschatological; that is God's Rule, the Kingdom of God, would erupt dynamically from above and during the lifetime of Jesus' contemporaries. That Jesus' prediction about the time of God's Rule was not fulfilled in his or the disciples' lifetime led Matthew and Luke to edit Mark 9:1.

Twelfth, it is now admitted that Jesus' parables are thoroughly Jewish and are paralleled by other ancient Jewish parables, especially those in Rabbinics. Foremost among recent publications is Flusser's *Die rabbinischen Gleichnisse und der Gleichniserzähler Jesus*.[62] Flusser's insights have been developed and made accessible to the English reader by his pupil, Brad Young, in *Jesus and His Jewish Parables*.[63] Still unexplored, and unknown to many scholars, are the striking parallels to Jesus' parables in the story (or parable) of the lame man and blind man in the

Jewish pseudepigraphon titled the Apocryphon of Ezekiel, which is eschatological, realistically attuned to actual life and nature, and focused on the impending last judgment (see the text in *Old Testament Pseudepigrapha*).

Thirteenth, the archaeology of pre-70 Palestine is now proving a major challenge and stimulus to Jesus Research. We must avoid sensational claims, the temptation to be apologetic, and the confusion between the evangelists' additions and traditions authentic to Jesus of Nazareth. These excesses mar Gaalyah Cornfeld's *The Historical Jesus: A Scholarly View of the Man and His World.*[64] Cornfeld is not a scholar like Ephraim E. Urbach, M. Stern, Shemaryahu Talmon, Daniel R. Schwartz, or David Flusser; and his book should be read with some caution.

In 1982 the perceptive and influential Jew Paul Winter saw the dawning of a new era in research and the emergence of Jesus Research. Note his valid insight that

> the last decade has seen an amazing transformation. Now, the Jesus of history seems more accessible than ever. Like archaeologists swarming over a prime location, the historians and theologians have turned with gusto to the original documents, parallel historical records and the geographical sites, and at every turn have found a clearer and clearer picture emerging of Jesus of Nazareth.[65]

Archaeological research has awakened us, for example, to the minute provisions taken to cleanse oneself ritualistically. The pre-70 houses in upper Jerusalem are replete with *mikvaot*, that is, Jewish baths for purification. Moreover, the large stone vessels found *in situ* inform us of the expenses taken to insure prevention of contamination from those who are impure. Clay vessels did not protect the contents inside from contamination, and this ruling is found not only in Rabbinics but also in the largest of the Dead Sea Scrolls, the Temple Scroll. Surely, Jesus' concept of purity was markedly different from these wealthy aristocrats living in Jerusalem. Should we not think that Jesus' concept of purity set him up on a collision course with the Jerusalem establishment? Obviously they would have been astounded by his edict that not what goes into the mouth contaminates but what comes out of it. Their position, power, and source of income were based on another interpretation of Torah.

Fourteenth, these observations lead us to stress the growing importance played in Jesus Research by sociology, anthropology, and some branches of psychology. The Oxford scholar A. E. Harvey attempted to show in *Jesus and the Constraints of History* that Jesus, like any great teacher, had to couch his proclamations within the constraints acceptable to his own particular social, historical, and linguistic setting.[66] We need to endeavor to understand the social world in which Jesus grew up and lived.

Fifteenth, nothing is so clear as the fact that Jesus was recognized as unusual because of the power and authority he claimed. In *The Charismatic Leader and His Followers* Hengel, the most influential German New Testament scholar today, argued for the unparalleled authority with which Jesus spoke. The unique way in which Jesus called others to follow him was an indication of his underivable "messianic" authority.[67] Hugh Anderson takes issue with some of Hengel's arguments. In particular, he finds it unlikely that "charismatic leader" adequately "embraces the whole of Jesus' being or of his authority. . . . " He concludes that although the christological perspectives of the early church certainly colored the accounts of Jesus' authority Jesus is best understood as "prophet or teacher extraordinary."[68]

Sixteenth, more and more scholars are coming to defend the possibility that Jesus thought of himself in terms of messianic and eschatological ideas. The Swede Ragnar Leivestad rightly points out that the proper means to discern Jesus' self-understanding (used here to connote Jesus' self-consciousness) is by exploring the possible impact of Jewish eschatological and messianic beliefs upon him.[69]

Seventeenth, more and more scholars acknowledge the importance of Jesus' miracles and acknowledge that many of the healing miracles are authentic. Surely if his opponents claim he performed miracles because he was possessed of a demon — which is certainly a reliable tradition preserved in Mark 3:22 — then they did not deny that he performed miracles. Following the lead of Fiebig and Vermes many experts are attempting to understand Jesus in terms of the Galilean miracle workers like Honi and Hanini ben Dosa.

Eighteenth, it is now widely recognized that Jesus began his ministry with John the Baptizer and that he tended to couch his message in eschatological tones similar to those of his former teacher. Recently Boers stressed the significance of John for Jesus. He inherited the concept of the Kingdom of God from John. In *Who Was Jesus?* Boers urges us not to lose "the tension created by the paradox of his relationship to John, which alone provides the framework within which his real significance is recognizable" (49).

Nineteenth, scholars have tended to conclude that Jesus did not belong to the Pharisees, Zealots, or Essenes; he had clashes with all known Jewish groups. In *Jesus von Nazareth im Lichte der jüdischen Gruppenbildung* Günther Baumbach shows that Jesus collided with Pharisees, Sadducees, Sicarii, and Zealots.[70] As W. S. LaSor and so many other specialists have shown,[71] Jesus was not an Essene and would have clashed with their strict interpretation of Torah, elevated concept of ritualistic purification, and separation from others. Despite Sanders's attempt to show that Jesus was not opposed to the Pharisees,[72] most scholars would tend to agree with John Bowker, who in *Jesus and the Pharisees*[73] argued that Jesus was a rebel who opposed extremists like some of the Pharisees.

Jesus shared much with the Pharisee Hillel, but his arguments with the Pharisees cannot be easily recast so that he differed only with the Shammaite branch of Pharisaism, even though this attempt was made in 1985 by Rabbi Harvey Falk in *Jesus the Pharisee: A New Look at the Jewishness of Jesus.*[74] It is difficult to reconstruct the life and teachings of Hillel. The transmission of his traditions received adulation and embellishment similar to the Jesus traditions (with the caveat, of course, that he was not deified and

worshipped). The relation between Hillel and Jesus, and
between the house of Hillel and the schools of Matthew
and John, is assessed by a group of international experts in
the forthcoming book *Hillel and Jesus*.[75]

In the late 1960s and early 1970s many scholars were
convinced that Jesus should be linked with the Zealots and
that he wanted to overthrow Rome. This position was developed by S. G. F. Brandon in his *Jesus and the Zealots;*
he did not think that Jesus himself was a Zealot, but the
presence of Simon the Zealot in his group convinced the
Romans that he was a revolutionary.[76] Now Hernando
Guevara in "La resistencia judía contra Roma en la época
de Jesús"[77] demonstrates why Jesus should not be portrayed as a Zealot. Most scholars would tend to agree with
this conclusion and accept it as already well established.[78]

While some journalists have claimed that Jesus was an
Essene and may have lived among the Jews who composed
the Dead Sea Scrolls, New Testament experts hesitate to
make such a categorical statement. They have acknowledged the striking links between Jesus and the Essenes.
Some scholars have attributed these similarities to the
influence of converted Essenes in the Palestinian Jesus
movement. Others have seen possible contacts between
Jesus and the Essenes. Still others, most notably the great
Israeli scholar Yigael Yadin, conclude that Jesus was anti-
Essene.[79] The explosion of interest in the Dead Sea Scrolls,
obviously related to the opening up of the so-called car-
tel that has monopolized Qumran research since the 1950s,
brings into central focus the question, How and in what
ways, if at all, was the historical Jesus influenced by the Essenes, the authors of the Dead Sea Scrolls? The consensus is
clarified and new explorations shared in *Jesus and the Dead
Sea Scrolls*.[80]

Finally, Jesus was sometimes disturbingly offensive, as
F. F. Bruce demonstrated in his balanced study, *The Hard
Sayings of Jesus*.[81] In *The Charismatic Leader and His Followers* Hengel examined Jesus' incredibly offensive retort to
the would-be follower of Jesus who needed first to bury

his father: "Let the dead bury the dead."[82] In *Difficult Sayings in the Gospels* Robert H. Stein discusses and seeks to understand Jesus' use of exaggerated language.[83]

In summary, we must recognize that the church needs to be aware of the perennial tendency to confess Jesus' uniqueness, equate him with God, and ignore his humanness. The heart of Christianity is the doctrine of the Incarnation. As the great Roman Catholic scholar Raymond E. Brown has shown in his *Jesus, God and Man: Modern Biblical Reflections*, we must boldly speak against the "widespread opposition to the humanity of Jesus."[84] God is not dismissed in the New Testament; Jesus does not usurp God's throne. Nowhere in the New Testament or in Christian creeds or edicts is it affirmed that Jesus was blessed with perfect knowledge. Christians are challenged to contemplate not only Jesus' divinity but also his humanity.

We come much closer to the historical source and grounding of the Christian's faith when we observe the humor of Jesus as indicative of his real humanity. He could be entertaining and humorous. This factor of his life has been ignored because of a misplaced piety; it is now brought again into focus by the German Louis Kretz in *Witz, Humor und Ironie bei Jesus*[85] and by the Swede Jakob Jónsson in *Humour and Irony in the New Testament.*[86]

MAJOR CHALLENGES TO CONSENSUS

What significant challenges, if any, are being made to these twenty points of consensus (at least in my view of present research)? From an overview do we see, following Enoch's vision, something like shepherds who kill and destroy their own sheep (1 Enoch 89:69), or something like shepherds who are successfully "pasturing for twelve hours" (1 Enoch 89:72)?

Some of the points in the consensus have been challenged by a few excellent scholars. Four challenges to the consensus are significant; one demands a different

paradigm, another calls for a shift of emphasis, and the final two are basically additions to the methodology being
employed.

The Cynic Jesus

Some scholars have drawn attention to the Cynics and
claim that Jesus should be reunderstood in light of what
we know about them. The parallels between Jesus and the
Cynics was discussed by scholars long ago, and at the turn
of the century experts like Johannes Weiss urged students
of the New Testament to study Cynicism as well as Sto-
icism.[87] Bultmann wrote his dissertation on a comparison
of Paul's preaching style with the diatribe of the Cynics
and Stoics.[88] In 1936 E. Wechsler[89] and in 1954 Carl Schneider[90] noted a significant link between Jesus and the Cynics.
They wrote in the heyday of the history of religions school,
before the discovery and impact of the Dead Sea Scrolls,
which began to change the perception and reconstruction
of Early Judaism and especially earliest Christianity about
the time of Schneider's book.

The new interest in Cynicism began perhaps in 1976
with the publication of the supplementary volume to the
Interpreter's Dictionary of the Bible. While the *IDB* did not
contain an entry on the Cynics the *IDBS* did; and it was
by Abraham J. Malherbe (201–3). He saw no link between Jesus and the Cynics, although he drew parallels
between them and Paul and concluded that these similarities "illustrate how Hellenistic philosophy contributed
to a congenial climate for the transmission of early Christianity."[91] Malherbe continued his interest in the Cynics
by publishing in 1977 *The Cynic Epistles: A Study Edition*[92]
and in the same year *Social Aspects of Early Christianity.*[93] In
the latter book he observes that "the highly individualistic
Cynics" probably did not have "organized communities"
(14). He then warns against the tendency to attribute to
the Cynics social habits that are foreign to them. He again
makes observations regarding Paul and the Cynics (49,

90n). In 1970 he published an article on the importance of the Cynics for understanding Paul's 1 Thessalonians;[94] but again he does not point to parallels between Jesus and the Cynics.[95]

In 1977, the year in which Malherbe's two works appeared, Gerd Theissen published an attempt to use sociology to reconstruct the Jesus movement in Palestine. He argued that Jesus' followers were "wandering charismatics" and that they were "in some way analogous" to the Cynic philosophers. Both led a vagabond existence, renouncing "home, families and possessions."[96] Theissen was forced to admit that the Jesus movement was in Palestine, but the parallels to the Cynics took him "outside Palestine" (15).[97]

In attempting to discern if references to the Cynics are fruitful in Jesus Research it is imperative not to confuse Jesus with his followers, Jesus with Paul, the members of the Palestinian Jesus group with Paul or the later authors of the post-Pauline epistles.[98] In this task we are aided not only by Malherbe's handy edition and translation of the Cynics, but also in 1988 with F. Gerald Downing's *Christ and the Cynics: Jesus and Other Radical Preachers in First-Century Tradition*.[99] Downing himself stresses that while the "traditions about Jesus" are "Palestinian Jewish," the "first Christian missionaries" would have "looked like a kind of Cynic" (v–vi). Downing is urging us, however, to rethink the Jesus traditions themselves and to allow for similarities between Jesus' preaching and the Cynic traditions. Rejecting the explanation that the parallels with the Cynics derive from Jesus' interpreters, the first Christian missionaries, Downing boldly claims that the "Cynic colour is the colour Jesus of Nazareth himself gave to his teaching."[100] Downing, as Theissen earlier, had to admit that we have no evidence of Cynics in Palestine during Jesus' day. His appeal to Sepphoris is not far-fetched, but it is an argument from silence. There is presently, as far as I know, no evidence of Cynics in Jesus' milieu; and archaeologists have found no evidence of Cynics in pre-70 Palestine.[101]

The major stimulus to seek Jesus in terms of the Cynics and not in terms of Jewish traditions is Burton L. Mack. In 1988 in *A Myth of Innocence* Mack claimed that "not only Jesus' style of social criticism," but also "his themes and topics are much closer to Cynic idiom than to those characteristic for public Jewish piety. One seeks in vain a direct engagement of specifically Jewish concerns."[102] Mack is thus not only pushing the Cynic connection; he is also denying the links between Jesus and Judaism. Note these words: "The Cynic analogy repositions the historical Jesus away from a specifically Jewish sectarian milieu and toward the Hellenistic ethos known to have prevailed in Galilee."[103]

Mack's sweeping generalizations are not supported by careful analysis and exegesis. His reconstruction of pre-70 Galilee is not harmonious with the evidence that has been supplied by Meyers and Strange[104] or discussed in the volumes on Galilee by Freyne and Levine.[105] It is significant that none of Malherbe's students have argued that Jesus was a Cynic or influenced by Cynicism; this observation is all the more striking since they issued a Festschrift for him in 1990.[106]

Too often apparent similarities are accorded significance that they do not warrant. Parallels are without force until context and intent is carefully assessed. In *Sociology and the Jesus Movement* Richard A. Horsley insightfully shows that parallels between the Cynics and Luke 10:4 do not suggest Cynic influence. After Jesus states that he is sending the seventy out "as lambs in the midst of wolves," the passage from Luke continues with the following injunction: "Carry no purse, no bag, no sandals; and salute no one on the road." This verse has been taken as evidence of Cynic influence on Jesus, or at least on an early community of his followers (the Q community).[107] Horsley rightly points out that the contrasts between Jesus and the Cynics are evident in this exhortation. The "prohibition of a wallet does not conform to the typical description of the Cynic, who proverbially wore a *pera*, which supposedly indicated his self-sufficiency."[108] Whereas this saying of Jesus prohibits saluting another on the road, the "Cynics were famous for their so-called 'boldness of speech' " (117). Horsley concludes, "Thus, in three of its five prohibitions" the passage in Luke 10:4 "could thus be understood almost as *anti*-Cynic."[109]

It is evident that those who want to recast Jesus in light of the Cynics have not presented a convincing case. They may still be able to persuade some scholars, but they will have to explain the alleged parallels and demonstrate the evidence for Cynics in Palestine during the time of Jesus. They will also need to demonstrate that the Cynics were a social group in antiquity and not merely a generic term for social critics.[110] I am convinced they have failed on all these points.[111]

The Noneschatological Jesus

Marcus J. Borg achieved scholarly notice in the world of New Testament research in 1984 with the publication of his revised Oxford dissertation, *Conflict, Holiness and Politics in the Teachings of Jesus*.[112] Borg concluded that the historical Jesus was "a Jewish holy man and sage, in addition to being a prophet." What was significant about Borg's book was the focus he brought to Jesus by stressing the concept of holiness. That Jesus was not a Zealot does not mean he was "indifferent to politics."[113] Rightly stressing that multiple criteria and methods should be used, he argued that we should try to situate Jesus within his social context, which for him denoted "conflict as a context for interpreting the teaching of Jesus."[114] In contrast to the other Jewish concepts of holiness, Jesus "internalized holiness": "The way to purity of heart was not exclusively or even primarily through obedience to the Torah, but the path of dying to the self and the world."[115] This rather old interpretation has a new ring in Borg's work. For him what is new are the implications derived from Jesus' social setting. Holiness did not mean driving the Romans out of Palestine

(as it did in the Psalms of Solomon and the early Zealots).
It did not mean withdrawal from society (as it did in the
Dead Sea Scrolls). It did not mean separation within society (as it did to many Sadducees, some Pharisees, the
community behind the Temple Scroll, and the Jewish aristocrats living in upper Jerusalem). For Borg Jesus' concept
of holiness had "political implications" because his culture
was on "a collision course with Rome." Borg's insights are
generally persuasive; they are a significant contribution to
recovering the historical Jesus.[116]

It seems certain that in some ways Jesus' program for
restoring Israel had political dimensions and not merely
overtones. I find it odd that specialists on Jesus Research
admit that Jesus must be understood within Judaism and
that Jews did not separate politics from religion, and then
go on to claim that Jesus was not interested in politics.
Jesus certainly was not attempting to overthrow Rome
and establish a messianic kingdom in Jerusalem; but he
also could not have been oblivious to the political implications of his actions and teachings. The setting of Jesus
within first-century Jewish nationalism now receives a firm
founding in Mendels's *The Rise and Fall of Jewish Nationalism*, which is summarized and developed in the present
volume.[117]

The major question regarding Borg's presentation of
the historical Jesus concerns the place and meaning of the
Kingdom of God in the teaching of Jesus. Surely it would
be unwise to interpret the Kingdom of God as something
that was only a matter of the inward heart. Yet Borg defines
the Kingdom of God in the teaching of Jesus as "a symbol
for the presence and power of God as known in mystical
experience."[118] For Borg, "Jesus used the phrase Kingdom
of God within the framework of what we might call an eschatological mysticism (a mysticism which used language
associated with the end of the world) or a mystical eschatology (an eschatology in which the new age was the other
realm of mystical communion)."[119]

To use the word "mysticism" in terms of first-century

Jewish thought is fraught with difficulties and can be more confusing than clarifying. Even more important, Jesus used the phrase Kingdom of God "within the framework" of Jewish thought in which it appeared and was significantly developed, as we shall see. Borg has continued his work with the publication of an article titled "A Temperate Case for a Non-Eschatological Jesus,"[120] and especially in 1987 in his book, *Jesus: A New Vision*.[121] There is insufficient space to do full justice to Borg's research. It is careful, insightful, even polemical and apologetic. I fully agree with him that the evangelists' portraits of Jesus make eminent historical sense and that the concept of purity[122] is essential in understanding Jesus in his environment. It is obviously easy to agree with Borg that "the historical Jesus" is "a Spirit-filled figure in the charismatic stream of Judaism"[123] and that our own world is one that does not comprehend the "reality of the Spirit."

But are we involved in Jesus Research or seeking to reclaim Jesus for modern understanding and faith? If Schweitzer has not convinced New Testament scholars that Jesus' message was thoroughly apocalyptic, he probably did show persuasively to most experts that Jesus' concept of the Kingdom of God was not an "inward spiritual reality or a this-worldly social or ethical goal," to use the words of Dwight Moody Smith.[124]

Borg's Jesus seems so inoffensive and familiar. Yet why was Jesus crucified? And does not Jesus' end reveal something about his life?[125] I am persuaded that I have not created a Jesus who serves my faith but have been confronted by a historical figure when Jesus appears offensive and strange. And he does behave offensively in some passages in the New Testament — most notably in his rejection of a would-be follower with the retort that he should let the dead bury the dead.

Borg does not deal adequately with the sayings of Jesus that mention the Son of Man. Besides noting what other scholars have said about the meaning of these sayings Borg only advises that the "coming Son of Man"

sayings are not authentic to Jesus.[126] The attribution of
the Son of Man sayings entirely to the early church is
no longer feasible, despite the brilliance of Hans Conzelmann's *Jesus*, which in its day was representative of only
a few of Bultmann's extremely skeptical students.[127] The
English scholar Barnabas Lindars, in *Jesus: Son of Man*, illustrates why most experts recognize that some of the Son
of Man sayings in the Gospels are authentic and provide
us with important data for comprehending Jesus' understanding of his mission.[128] Very important books on the Son
of Man sayings have been published by A. J. B. Higgins
and Chrys C. Caragounis.[129] In 1990 D. R. A. Hare published his reflections of over fifteen years on this theme
under the title *The Son of Man Tradition*.[130] He concludes
that Jesus probably "regarded himself as Messiah, was
not an apocalyptist," and used *bar enasha* "as a modest
self-reference."[131]

The Canadian Roman Catholic New Testament expert
Ben F. Meyer is entirely correct to argue, in *The Aims
of Jesus*, that Jesus' focal point was proclaiming the imminence of God's Rule — the Kingdom of God.[132] Odo
Camponovo has recently examined the use of the Rule
of God (or Kingdom of God) and related terms and concepts in *Königtum, Königsherrschaft und Reich Gottes in den
Frühjüdischen Schriften*.[133] Helmut Merklein has clarified
Jesus' concept of God's kingdom in *Jesu Botschaft von der
Gottesherrschaft*.[134] Martin Hengel and A. M. Schwemer
have edited a Tübingen symposium that was focused on
the Kingdom of God in Judaism and early Christianity.[135]
In light of these and other publications,[136] I find something
essential missing in Borg's attempt to situate Jesus within
his time; and that fundamental dimension is the cosmol-
ogy and eschatology of Jesus' Jewish contemporaries in
Palestine. Jesus' fellow Jews were convinced that the world
was filled with good and evil spirits. Common mythology
portrayed Satan warring with Gabriel. For Jesus and his
contemporaries the air was charged with expectations that
the end of the world was about to occur. We have more lit-

erary evidence of these concerns during the time of Jesus than we did even a decade ago.[137] While it is clear that Jesus cannot be categorized as an apocalyptist, should we follow Borg in so de-eschatologizing him? I would like to, but what I know about his time and about the traditions that derive from him will not permit me to conclude in favor of a de-eschatologized Jesus.

Perhaps I have not fully understood Borg, because on almost every page of his books I find myself agreeing with him. Jesus was indeed "a charismatic healer, unconventional sage, and founder of an alternative community."[138] I am also in agreement with Martin Buber, the brilliant Jewish philosopher, who rightly perceived that there is something about Jesus that powerfully transcends Jewish concepts and categories.[139] How can Borg, however, claim that Jesus "warned of the fall of Jerusalem"[140] and still argue for a de-eschatologized Jesus? Borg is moving in the proper direction — in his essay contained in the present collection of symposium papers — to stress that when he uses the term "eschatological expectation" with regard to Jesus he means near-end expectation, or an *imminent* apocalyptic eschatology.

I would prefer to argue that some of Jesus' sayings are clearly eschatological but that not everything he taught was tinged by eschatology. For example, his fondness for children and exhortation to let them come to him is not an eschatological pronouncement and may have been anti-eschatological. His parable of the ten maidens (Matt. 25:1–13) seems to go back to him (*mutatis mutandis*), and its essential message is to be prepared to wait for the coming of God's Rule on earth.

The Extracanonical Jesus

The third challenge is to add to Jesus Research much more from the extracanonical Christian literature. This endeavor has recent roots in Joachim Jeremias's works, and in books by Bruce, Wenham, Stroker, Helmut Koester, and others.[141]

The explosion of recent interest in the New Testament Apocrypha and Pseudepigrapha was illustrated in my *The New Testament Apocrypha and Pseudepigrapha*.[142]

The most exciting challenge comes from John Dominic Crossan. In numerous books he claims that Jesus Research must be enriched and corrected by an examination of the extracanonical writings. His most sensational claim is that the Gospel of Peter preserves an ancient tradition that antedated and informed the evangelists Mark, Matthew, Luke, and John. This argument is presented in Crossan's *Four Other Gospels: Shadows on the Contours of the Canon*.[143]

Crossan's claims are often excessive; they may even retard the movement to study sensitively the antiquity of the traditions in the apocryphal gospels (as they apparently have for Raymond E. Brown and John P. Meier).[144] We need to overcome our bias in favor of the canonical Gospels as the only repository of reliable traditions. While the antiquity and probable independence of the Gospel of Thomas and the Gospel of Peter are being affirmed, the editorial and expansive nature of the canonical Gospels is being accepted as assured results of research. The so-called extracanonical works are therefore a rich field for exploration. Dwight Moody Smith, for example, examines the relation between John and the synoptics in terms of the apocryphal traditions and the obvious oral tradition that was alive until at least Papias's time at the beginning of the second century.[145] The New Testament Apocrypha and Pseudepigrapha are available for renewed intensive research thanks to the republication of a new edition of the major collection.[146]

The Jesus of Sociology

Surely one of the most exciting and enriching areas for research is being provided by stimuli deriving from a sociologically sensitive examination of Jesus' life. Following Weber, Hengel has shown that "charisma" is an appropriate category for Jesus.[147] Theissen's early attempt to

describe the social world of Jesus' earliest followers stimulated much subsequent work; but it was vitiated by too
much dependence on a functionalism that is fraught with
difficulties, as Horsley has demonstrated.[148] Douglas E.
Oakman's *Jesus and the Economic Questions of His Day*[149]
contains rich insights for a better appreciation of Jesus'
society.

In 1985 in *Bandits, Prophets, and Messiahs: Popular Movements at the Time of Jesus* and in 1987 in *Jesus and the
Spiral of Violence: Popular Jewish Resistance in Roman Palestine*
Horsley has demonstrated that the theological approach
to Jesus and his time has failed and that since such work
is historical research it must be pursued according to the
highest standards of historiography. He wisely urges us to
use sociology, or at least sociological sensitivities, in exploring Jesus' time. He then boldly attempts to reconstruct
Jesus' life and message. Horsley is probably correct and
Sanders incorrect in arguing that Jesus was at times in conflict with the Pharisees. He concludes a reconstruction of
Jesus' message by contending that Jesus intended to restore
meaning in the local communities of Galilee:

> ...in response to illness, self-blame, and possession by
> alien spiritual forces, for example, the Jesus movement
> continued the healing, forgiveness of sin, and exorcism
> initiated by Jesus. In attempting to deal with the heavy in-
> debtedness, poverty, and despair that plagued many of the
> people, the Jesus movement advocated mutual forgiveness
> of debts, social-economic cooperation, and other forms of
> reciprocity in local communities.[150]

Certainly this reconstruction is at once challenging and
perplexing. Was Jesus interested in only a portion of Israel? Did he not exhort his disciples to go into the villages
of Israel? Did he not appoint twelve to rule over each of
the tribes of Israel? Can we cavalierly treat the traditions
in John that report extensive and frequent stays by Jesus in
and around Jerusalem?

Obviously the best attempts to reconstruct Jesus and
his time must be informed by sociology. That does not

mean we can simply employ one sociological insight or
method and reconstruct the past. Sociology has no method
with which to study texts or the past. Sociologists like Weber and Durkheim[151] and their students can help us be
sensitive to problems in understanding communities and
societies. Obviously many methods employed by sociologists should be used, and then we need to be self-critical.
The best book on how to proceed in this process is probably Bengt Holmberg's *Sociology and the New Testament*.[152]
Holmberg does not attempt to reconstruct Jesus' time but
explains how to lay a foundation for such work. He rightly
sees the function of sociology as providing models that will
help us raise new questions and derive new insights.

In over two hundred books the American Jewish expert Jacob Neusner has demonstrated that the Jewish
world of Jesus' time was torn by multiple competing
claims. He correctly points out that "Jesus came into a
world of irrepressible conflict."[153] This insight is helpful
as we seek to discern the conflicts Jesus could not escape,
those he chose to engage, and those that ultimately cost
him death by crucifixion.

In this endeavor we must improve upon Horsley's
reconstruction, pruning it of the disparagement of Jewish apocalypticism. It simply is not correct to report that
"there is no evidence of a pervasive apocalypticism in ancient Jewish Palestine."[154] Virtually every Jewish writing
we have from about the time of Jesus that is Palestinian
is apocalyptic or influenced in some way by Jewish apocalypticism. This is true for the Dead Sea Scrolls, the Pseudepigrapha, Paul's letters, and much of the early Gospel
tradition. The assessment of messianism in Early Judaism,
especially in the first century C.E. and in the life of Jesus
and his followers, is now thoroughly discussed by a group
of international experts in the reference work titled *The
Messiah*.[155]

Horsley's reconstruction also needs to be supple-
mented with insights obtained from other sociological
approaches. Mary Douglas's *Purity and Danger* helps clar-

ify the ways we can comprehend the dangers Jesus faced, since they were often related to the heightened degree of holiness demanded and the absolute boundaries set, especially by the Jerusalem-based priests and scribes.[156] Victor Turner's marvelous work *Process, Performance and Pilgrimage: A Study in Comparative Symbology*[157] and his "Pilgrimages as Social Processes"[158] are full of insights that will help us understand Jesus' last trip to Jerusalem, since Jesus and his entourage clearly went up to Jerusalem at the prescribed time for the Passover pilgrimage.

CONCLUSION

We now come to the end of a terrifyingly rapid review of Jesus Research today. I have chosen to focus on what seem to me to be the major developments and challenges in this area of study. It is certainly apparent that any contribution to our attempts to reconstruct the past, especially of Jesus and his time, demands focusing, and this necessary choice means to limit the scope of view. As Maurice Merleau-Ponty demonstrated, to focus on a particular is to become blind to the whole.[159] That caveat means that we must focus in order to see, but we must also step back, take a general overview, refocus, correct the distortion caused by myopia, and then attempt to obtain a representative perception from multiple attempts at focusing, absorbing the view, and refocusing again to grasp the correct perception.

What is our final perspective on current research? Are we to think, again with Enoch, of sheep, who have finally become "all snow-white" with magnificent wool, gentle, and with eyes now open, being gathered together and returning to the great house (1 Enoch 90:32–36)?

Long ago Ernst Käsemann, perhaps the most brilliant of Bultmann's students, urged us to comprehend, in seeking to discern what can be known with some probability about Jesus of Nazareth, to reflect on how we can know history. He wisely pointed out that history is accessible only through tradition and understandable only through selection and interpretation.[160] Käsemann, in *Der Ruf der Freiheit*, persuasively saw that one of the problems with which we must struggle is to discern, "in so far as there ever was anything here to discuss, whether and why the devout man [Jesus] was 'liberal.'"[161]

As Nils Dahl so brilliantly stated in *Jesus in the Memory of the Early Church*, the "gospel is intended to be a witness and thereby an inspired 'commemoration' of the life and work of Jesus, in which everything radiates with the light of the resurrection."[162] Especially for those who are overly influenced by Martin Kähler's and Bultmann's insistence on the creative powers of the post-Easter Jesus community, the key word is "commemoration." Jesus' early followers remembered him and the years together with him in Galilee and Judaea, and their memory was not so unreliable as scholars thought during the middle of the present century. As John Maier, Willi Marxsen, and C. F. D. Moule stress in their erudite works,[163] the separation of the Christ of faith from the Jesus of history results from a false dichotomy; the earliest christologies were frequently grounded in Jesus' own words and self-understanding.

The task of Christian scholars is to live and study in close contact with Jesus of Nazareth in order to grasp his authentic message and to re-present it to all in the present day.[164] This endeavor entails attempting to breathe the Jewish spirit that awakened Jesus. As the Sterling Professor of History at Yale, Jaroslav Pelikan, states in his magisterial *Jesus through the Centuries*, the "first attempts to understand and interpret his message took place within the context of Judaism, and it is likewise there that any attempt to understand his place in the history of human culture must begin."[165] Once we recognize that behind the various kerygmata of Jesus' earliest followers lies the unassailable historicity of the man Jesus of Nazareth, then we can comprehend Schillebeeckx's insight that this Jesus is "the one and only basis for an authentic Christology."[166] In a similar vein Paula Fredriksen wisely concludes that the church, "by claiming faith in Jesus as the unique occasion of divine revelation, thus lays upon itself the obligation to do history."[167]

After his long and complicated vision of the shepherds and the sheep Enoch reports: "Then I woke up and blessed the Lord of righteousness and gave him glory" (1 Enoch 90:40). There is no better way to glorify God than by honest inquiry into how and in what ways it is possible today — with vast new primary sources and enriched and improved methodologies — to reconstruct the life and teachings of the one whom Christians affirm as their Lord.[168] Journalists continue to misrepresent the study of Jesus in his time by dedicated Christians and Jews; they — and all the readers of the essays in this volume know — that there is more than one simple set of alternatives: "The Son of God, Or a Twice-Married Zealot Who Lived until 70?"[169]

NOTES

1. See James H. Charlesworth, ed., *The Old Testament Pseudepigrapha*, 2 vols. (Garden City, N.Y.: Doubleday, 1983, 1985).

2. Hugh Anderson, *Jesus* (Englewood Cliffs, N.J.: Prentice-Hall, 1967), 16.

3. Burton L. Mack, *A Myth of Innocence: Mark and Christian Origins* (Philadelphia: Fortress, 1988).

4. See David E. Aune, "The Prophetic Role of Jesus," and "The Prophecies of Jesus" in *Early Christianity and the Ancient Mediterranean World* (Grand Rapids, 1983), 153–88. Also see David E. Aune, *Prophecy in Early Christianity and the Ancient Mediterranean World* (Grand Rapids: Eerdmans, 1983). David Hill, "Jesus: 'A Prophet Mighty in Deed and Word,'" in *New Testament Prophecy* (Atlanta: John Knox, 1979), 48–69.

5. See E. P. Sanders, *Jesus and Judaism* (Philadelphia: Fortress, 1985), 124, 152. Christopher Rowland, *The Open Heaven: The Study of Apocalyptic in Judaism and Early Christianity* (New York: Crossroad, 1982). J. D. G. Dunn, *Jesus and the Spirit: A Study of the Religious and Charismatic Experience of Jesus and the First Christians as Reflected in the New Testament* (Philadelphia: Westminster, 1975).

6. Marcus J. Borg, *Conflict, Holiness and Politics in the Teachings of Jesus*, Studies in the Bible and Early Christianity 5 (Lewiston, N.Y.: Edwin Mellen, 1984). Also see Borg, "The Teaching of Jesus Christ," *Anchor Bible Dictionary* (1992), 3:804–12.

7. See especially Bruno Bauer, *Kritik der Evangelien*, 2 vols. (Berlin, 1850–51). For a sensitive and insightful critique of Bauer see Albert Schweitzer, *The Quest of the Historical Jesus*, trans. W. Montgomery, 2d ed. (London, 1931), 137–60. Also see P.-L. Couchoud, *The Creation of Christ: An Outline of the Beginnings of Christianity*, trans. C. B. Bonner (London, 1939); and the criticism of him by Maurice Goguel, *Jesus the Nazarene: Myth or History?* trans. F. Stephens (New York, 1926).

8. G. A. Wells, *Who Was Jesus? A Critique of the New Testament Record* (La Salle, Ill.: Open Court, 1989).

9. Ibid., 39–40.

10. G. A. Wells, "The Historicity of Jesus," in *Jesus in History and Myth*, ed. R. Joseph Hoffmann and Gerald A. Larue (New York: Prometheus Books, 1986), 27.

11. Hendrikus Boers, *Who Was Jesus?: The Historical Jesus and the Synoptic Gospels* (San Francisco: Harper San Francisco, 1989), 93.

12. P. M. Beaude, *Jésus de Nazareth*, Bibliothèque d'histoire du Christianisme 5 (Paris, 1983).

13. Herbert Leroy, *Jesus: Überlieferung und Deutung*, Erträge der Forschung 95 (Darmstadt, 1978). This book reviews the research on the historical Jesus from Albert Schweitzer to the 1970s.

14. Warren S. Kissinger, *The Lives of Jesus: A History and Bibliography* (New York: Garland, 1985).

15. A student's version, focused on publications in English, was recently printed; see Craig A. Evans, *Jesus*, IBR Bibliographies No. 5 (Grand Rapids: Baker Book House, 1992).

16. John Reumann, "Jesus and Christology," in *The New Testament and Its Modern Interpreters*, ed. Eldon J. Epp and George W. MacRae (Atlanta: Scholars Press, 1989), 501–64.

17. John P. Meier, "Reflections on Jesus-of-History Research Today," in James H. Charlesworth, ed., *Jesus' Jewishness: Exploring the Place of Jesus within Early Judaism* (New York: Crossroad, 1991), 84–107. See also his *A Marginal Jew: Rethinking the Historical Jesus*, Anchor Bible Reference Library (New York: Doubleday, 1991).

18. H. Stewart Chamberlain, *Foundations of the Nineteenth Century*, trans. John Lees, 2 vols. (New York: John Lane Co., 1910), 202–12.

19. David Flusser, *Jesus*, trans. R. Walls (New York, 1969); Flusser, *Judaism and the Origins of Christianity* (Jerusalem, 1988).

20. See also Sanders's *Jewish Law from Jesus to the Mishnah: Five Studies* (Philadelphia: Trinity Press International, 1990), especially see 90–96; also Sanders's *Judaism: Practice and Belief 63 BCE–63 CE* (Philadelphia: Trinity Press International, 1991), especially 257–60.

21. James S. Stewart, *The Life and Teaching of Jesus Christ* (Edinburgh, 1933, 1957 [2d ed.], 1977 [with amendments], 1981), 1.

22. Günther Bornkamm, *Jesus of Nazareth*, trans. Irene and Fraser McLuskey with James M. Robinson (New York: Harper, 1960).

23. Sanders, *Jesus and Judaism*, 2.

24. Rudolf Bultmann, *Theology of the New Testament*, trans. Kendrick Grobel, 2 vols. (New York, 1951, 1955), 1:3. In contrast to Bultmann, Joachim Jeremias in *New Testament Theology: The Proclamation of Jesus*, trans. John Bowden (New York, 1971) and Leonard Goppelt in *Theology of the New Testament*, trans. John E. Alsup, 2 vols. (Grand Rapids: Eerdmans, 1981, 1982) included the teachings of Jesus within New Testament theology.

25. Rudolf Bultmann, *Jesus and the Word*, trans. Louise Pettibone Smith and Erminie Huntress Lantero (London, 1958), 14.

26. See Bultmann, "The Primitive Christian Kerygma and the Historical Jesus," in *The Historical Jesus and the Kerygmatic Christ*, ed. and trans. Carl E. Braaten and R. A. Harrisville (New York, 1964); especially see p. 26, on which he emphasizes that Christian proclamation of Jesus as Lord is not subservient to scientific research, because the latter "puts to the kerygma a question with which it is not at all concerned."

27. *Jesus*, 18.

28. John Painter, *Theology as Hermeneutics: Rudolf Bultmann's Interpretation of the History of Jesus* (Sheffield, 1987), viii–ix.

29. David Flusser, *Jesus*, 7. This quotation, virtually unchanged, appears also in Charlesworth, ed., *Jesus' Jewishness*, 153.

30. William R. Farmer, *Jesus and the Gospel: Tradition, Scripture, and Canon* (Philadelphia: Fortress, 1982), 21.

31. Käsemann is extremely important because he openly challenged his teacher, Bultmann, and demonstrated that there is far more reliable historical information in the Gospels than he had indicated in the classroom and through publications and that this information is not irrelevant for Christian faith. See Käsemann, "The Problem of the Historical Jesus," in *Essays on New Testament Themes*, trans. W. J. Montague (Philadelphia,

1982), 15–47. Also see Käsemann, "Blind Alleys in the 'Jesus of History' Controversy," in *New Testament Questions of Today,* trans. W. J. Montague (Philadelphia: Fortress, 1969), 23–65; and Käsemann, "The Jesus Tradition as Access to Christian Origins," in *Colloquium: The Australian and New Zealand Theological Review* 13 (1981).

32. In addition to the bibliographical data supplied previously and by Craig A. Evans in *Life of Jesus Research,* see the following: J. C. O'Neill, *Messiah: Six Lectures on the Ministry of Jesus: The Cunningham Lectures 1975–76* (Cambridge, 1980, 1984). Doron Mendels, *The Rise and Fall of Jewish Nationalism: Jewish and Christian Ethnicity in Ancient Palestine,* Anchor Bible Reference Library (New York: Doubleday, 1992); Cardinal Carlo Maria Martini, "Christianity and Judaism: A Historical and Theological Overview," in *Jews and Christians: Exploring the Past, Present, and Future,* ed. James H. Charlesworth (New York: Crossroad, 1990), 19–26; P. Sacchi, "Jesus' Formative Background," in *Jesus and the Dead Sea Scrolls,* James H. Charlesworth, ed., Anchor Bible Reference Library (New York: Doubleday, 1993), 123–39; Daniel R. Schwartz, *Studies in the Jewish Background of Christianity,* Wissenschaftliche Untersuchungen zum Neuen Testament 60 (Tübingen: J. C. B. Mohr, 1992).

33. Michael Ramsey, *Jesus and the Living Past: The Hale Lectures 1978* (Oxford, New York: Oxford University Press, 1980).

34. A. E. Harvey, *God Incarnate* (London, 1981), 6.

35. Gustaf Aulén, *Jesus in Contemporary Historical Research,* trans. I. H. Hjelm (Philadelphia: Fortress, 1976), viii.

36. J. D. G. Dunn, *The Evidence for Jesus* (Philadelphia: Westminster, 1985).

37. Juan Luis Segundo, *The Historical Jesus of the Synoptics,* trans. John Drury, Jesus of Nazareth Yesterday and Today 2 (Maryknoll, N.Y.: Orbis Books, 1985).

38. For the works in mind, see especially B. D. Chilton, *A Galilean Rabbi and His Bible: Jesus' Use of the Interpreted Scripture of His Time,* Good News Studies 8 (Wilmington, Del.: Michael Glazier, 1984); A. E. Harvey, *Jesus and the Constraints of History* (Philadelphia, 1982). Also see the chapters in the present book by Borg, Horsley, and Mendels, and the citations in the following notes.

39. Leander E. Keck, *A Future for the Historical Jesus: The Place of Jesus in Preaching and Teaching* (New York, 1971), 33.

40. Charlesworth, *Jesus within Judaism,* 136–39.

41. Sanders, *Jesus and Judaism,* 100–101.

42. Gerhard Lohfink, *Jesus and Community: The Social Di-*

mension of Christian Faith, trans. J. P. Galvin (New York: Paulist, 1985), 10.

43. See, e.g., Jacob Neusner, "Money-Changers in the Temple: The Mishna's Explanation," *New Testament Studies* 35 (1989): 287–90. Craig A. Evans, "Jesus' Action in the Temple: Cleansing or Portent of Destruction," *Catholic Biblical Quarterly* 51 (1989): 237–70.

44. Sanders, *Jesus and Judaism*, 302.

45. Borg, *Conflict*.

46. Sean Freyne, *Galilee, Jesus and the Gospels: Literary Approaches and Historical Investigations* (Philadelphia: Fortress, 1988). Also see Freyne, "Galilee (Hellenistic/Roman)," *Anchor Bible Dictionary* (1992), 2:895–99.

47. Sherman E. Johnson, *Jesus and His Towns* (Wilmington, Del.: Michael Glazier, 1989).

48. Lee I. Levine, ed., *The Galilee in Late Antiquity* (New York: Jewish Theological Seminary of America, 1992).

49. B. Pixner, *With Jesus through Galilee according to the Fifth Gospel*, trans. C. Botha and D. Foster (Rosh Pina, 1992).

50. See especially Psalms of Solomon 17:21–25.

51. See Hyam Maccoby, *Judas Iscariot and the Myth of Jewish Evil* (New York: Free Press, 1992).

52. See James H. Charlesworth, "Pilate, Caiaphas, and Jesus' Trial," *Explorations* (forthcoming).

53. See Flusser's articles on Jesus in *Judaism and the Origins of Christianity*, passim.

54. Sanders, *Jewish Law from Jesus to the Mishnah*, 90–96.

55. Herbert Braun, *Jesus: Der Mann aus Nazareth und seine Zeit* (Stuttgart: Kreuz-Verlag, 1984). This revised German book is considerably improved over the 1969 work, which was translated into English: *Jesus of Nazareth: The Man and His Time*, trans. E. R. Kalin (Philadelphia: Fortress Press, 1979).

56. See especially the chapters titled "Jesus and the Old Testament Pseudepigrapha" (30–53) and "Jesus and the Dead Sea Scrolls" (54–75).

57. James H. Charlesworth, ed., *Jesus' Jewishness: Exploring the Place of Jesus within Early Judaism* (New York: Crossroad, 1991); James H. Charlesworth, ed., *Jesus and the Dead Sea Scrolls*, Anchor Bible Reference Library (New York: Doubleday, 1993).

58. Johannes Weiss, *Jesus' Proclamation of the Kingdom of God*, ed. and trans. R. H. Hiers and D. L. Holland (Philadelphia: Fortress, 1971).

59. Schweitzer, *The Quest of the Historical Jesus*.

60. Norman Perrin, *The Kingdom of God in the Teaching of Jesus* (Philadelphia: Westminster Press, 1963).

61. Howard Clark Kee, *Jesus in History: An Approach to the Study of the Gospels*, 2d ed. (New York: Harcourt Brace Javonovich, 1977).

62. David Flusser, *Die rabbinischen Gleichnisse und der Gleichniserzähler Jesus*, Judaica et Christiana 4 (Bern: Peter Lang, 1981).

63. Brad Young, *Jesus and His Jewish Parables* (New York: Paulist Press, 1989).

64. Gaalyah Cornfeld, *The Historical Jesus: A Scholarly View of the Man and His World* (New York: Macmillan, 1982).

65. Paul Winter, *The Search for the Real Jesus* (London, 1982). See also Winter's masterpiece titled *On the Trial of Jesus*, 2d ed., Studia Judaica 1 (Berlin, New York: De Gruyter, 1974).

66. A. E. Harvey, *Jesus and the Constraints of History* (Philadelphia, 1972).

67. Martin Hengel, *The Charismatic Leader and His Followers*, trans. J. C. G. Gried (New York: Crossroad, 1981).

68. Hugh Anderson, "Jesus: Aspects of the Question of His Authority," in *The Social World of Formative Christianity and Judaism*, ed. Jacob Neusner et al. (Philadelphia: Fortress, 1988), 290–310.

69. Ragnar Leivestad, "Jesus–Messias–Menschensohn: Die jüdischen Heilandserwartungen zur Zeit der ersten römischen Kaiser und die Frage nach dem messianischen Selbstbewusstsein Jesu," *Aufstieg und Niedergang der Römischen Welt* 25, no. 1 (1984): 220–64.

70. Günther Baumbach, *Jesus von Nazareth im Lichte der jüdischen Gruppenbildung* (Berlin: Evangelische Verlagsanstalt, 1971).

71. W. S. LaSor, *Dead Sea Scrolls and the New Testament* (Grand Rapids, 1972). Also see the contributions in Charlesworth, ed., *Jesus and the Dead Sea Scrolls.*

72. Sanders, *Jesus and Judaism*, 276–77, and *Jewish Law*, 95–96.

73. John Bowker, *Jesus and the Pharisees* (Cambridge: Cambridge University Press, 1973).

74. Harvey Falk, *Jesus the Pharisee: A New Look at the Jewishness of Jesus* (New York: Paulist, 1985).

75. James H. Charlesworth, ed., *Hillel and Jesus* (Minneapolis: Fortress, forthcoming).

76. S. G. F. Brandon, *Jesus and the Zealots: A Study of the Political Factor in Primitive Christianity* (New York: Charles Scribner's Sons, 1967).

77. Ph.D. dissertation, Rome, 1981.

78. See especially the following: Oscar Cullmann, *Jesus and the Revolutionaries*, trans. Gareth Putnam (New York: Harper & Row, 1970); Martin Hengel, *The Zealots*, trans. David Smith (Edinburgh: T. & T. Clark, 1989); Martin Hengel, *Victory over Violence: Jesus and the Revolutionists*, trans. D. E. Green (Philadelphia: Fortress Press, 1973).

79. Yigael Yadin, *The Temple Scroll: The Hidden Law of the Dead Sea Sect* (New York: Random House, 1985), 24–42.

80. Charlesworth, ed., *Jesus and the Dead Sea Scrolls*.

81. F. F. Bruce, *The Hard Sayings of Jesus*, The Jesus Library (London, 1983).

82. Martin Hengel, *The Charismatic Leader and His Followers*, trans. J. C. G. Greig (New York: Crossroad, 1981).

83. Robert H. Stein, *Difficult Sayings in the Gospels: Jesus' Use of Overstatement and Hyperbole* (Grand Rapids: Baker Book House, 1985), 99.

84. Raymond E. Brown, *Jesus, God and Man: Modern Biblical Reflections* (New York, 1967), ix.

85. Louis Kretz, *Witz, Humor und Ironie bei Jesus*, 2d ed. (Freiburg im Olten: Walter, 1982).

86. Jakob Jónsson, *Humour and Irony in the New Testament: Illuminated by Parallels in Talmud and Midrash*, with a foreword by Krister Stendahl, Beihefte zur Zeitschrift für Religions- und Geistesgeschichte 28 (Leiden: Brill, 1985).

87. Abraham J. Malherbe, "Hellenistic Moralists and the New Testament," *Aufstieg und Niedergang der Römischen Welt* 3 (1977).

88. Bultmann, *Der Stil der paulinischen Predigt und die Kynisch-Stoische Diatribe* (Göttingen: Vandenhoeck & Ruprecht, 1910). See the important insights in Malherbe, "Greco-Roman Religion and Philosophy and the New Testament," in *The New Testament and its Modern Interpreters*, 3–26; especially 17. Again, Malherbe draws attention to ways the Cynics help us understand Paul — not Jesus (17).

89. E. Wechsler, *Hellas im Evangelium* (Berlin, 1936).

90. Carl Schneider, *Geistesgeschichte des antiken Christentums*, 2 vols. (Munich: Beck, 1954).

91. Abraham J. Malherbe, "Cynics," *Interpreter's Dictionary of the Bible, Supplementary Volume* (1976), 203.

92. Abraham J. Malherbe, *The Cynic Epistles: A Study Edition*, SBL Sources for Biblical Study 12 (Missoula, Mont.: Scholars Press, 1977).

93. Abraham J. Malherbe, *Social Aspects of Early Christianity* (Baton Rouge: Louisiana State University Press, 1977).

94. Abraham J. Malherbe, "Gentle as a Nurse: The Cynic Background of 1 Thess. 2," *Novum Testamentum* 12 (1970): 203–17.

95. In the Malherbe Festschrift the attention rightly is on Paul; there is no chapter on the historical Jesus. See David L. Balch, et al., eds., *Greeks, Romans, and Christians: Essays in Honor of Abraham J. Malherbe* (Minneapolis: Augsburg Fortress, 1990). See the helpful bibliography on Malherbe on 367–71.

96. Gerd Theissen, *Sociology of Early Palestinian Christianity*, trans. John Bowden (Philadelphia: Fortress, 1977), 15.

97. Theissen's position is unchanged in the latest German edition: *Soziologie der Jesusbewegung*, 3d ed., Theologische Existenz Heute 194 (Munich: Kaiser, 1981), 20.

98. Jesus Research must not be influenced by the appreciation of the Cynics by such early scholars of the church as Clement of Alexandria (150–ca. 215) and Gregory Nazianzus (329–89). See R. F. Hock, "Cynics," in *Anchor Bible Dictionary* (1992), 1:1221–26. This article also contains a helpful bibliography on the Cynics.

99. F. Gerald Downing, *Christ and the Cynics: Jesus and Other Radical Preachers in First-Century Tradition*, JSOT Manuals 4 (Sheffield: JSOT Press, 1988).

100. See also Downing's *Jesus and the Threat of Freedom* (Philadelphia: Trinity Press International, 1987).

101. I am grateful to David E. Aune and Lee I. Levine for helpful discussions. See Aune's paper on the Cynics and Jesus in the forthcoming book titled *Hillel and Jesus*. He shows that Jesus was not influenced by "the Cynics."

102. Mack, *A Myth of Innocence*, 73.

103. Ibid.

104. See especially James F. Strange, "Archaeology and the Religion of Judaism in Palestine," *Aufstieg und Niedergang der Römischen Welt* 19, no. 1 (1979): 646–85; and Eric M. Meyers, "The Cultural Setting of Galilee: The Case of Regionalism and Early Judaism," *Aufstieg und Niedergang der Römischen Welt* 19, no. 1 (1979): 686–702.

105. See the previous discussion on Galilee, and especially Levine's *The Galilee in Late Antiquity*.

106. See especially R. F. Hock, "A Dog in the Manger: The Cynic Cynulcus among Athenaeus's Deipnosophists," in *Greeks, Romans, and Christians*, 20–37.

107. See the following: the Ph.D. dissertation by L. Vaage, "Q: The Ethos and Ethics of an Itinerant Intelligence," Claremont

Graduate School, 1987. The Ph.D. dissertation by J. Tashjian, "The Social Setting of the Mission Charge in Q," Claremont Graduate School, 1987. Tashjian's "The Social Setting of the Q Mission: Three Dissertations," in *Society of Biblical Literature 1988 Seminar Papers*, ed. D. Lull (Atlanta, 1988), 636–44.

108. Richard A. Horsley, *Sociology and the Jesus Movement* (New York: Crossroad, 1989), 117.

109. Ibid.

110. I am persuaded by Aune's arguments that the Cynics were not a social group in antiquity. See his article on Jesus and the Cynics in *Hillel and Jesus*, forthcoming.

111. Far more persuasive and challenging is Richard Bauckham's attempt to ascertain the role of Jesus' relatives in Palestine after 30 C.E. and the discovery that Luke's genealogy and the Epistle of Jude apparently derive from the same circle. See Bauckham's *Jude and the Relatives of Jesus in the Early Church* (Edinburgh: T. & T. Clark, 1990).

112. Marcus J. Borg, *Conflict, Holiness and Politics in the Teachings of Jesus*, Studies in the Bible and Early Christianity 5 (Lewiston, N.Y.: Edwin Mellen, 1984). I have enjoyed reading Borg's work and using it in classes.

113. Ibid., 5.

114. Ibid., 24.

115. Ibid., 247.

116. See Borg's contribution in the present volume.

117. Doron Mendels, *The Rise and Fall of Jewish Nationalism: Jewish and Christian Ethnicity in Ancient Palestine*, Anchor Bible Reference Library (New York: Doubleday, 1992).

118. Borg, *Conflict*, 254.

119. Ibid., 261.

120. Borg, *Forum* 2, no. 3 (1986): 81–102. Also see Borg, "An Orthodoxy Reconsidered: The 'End-of-the-World Jesus,'" in *The Glory of Christ in the New Testament: Studies in Christology in Memory of George Bradford Caird*, ed. L. D. Hurst and N. T. Wright (Oxford: Oxford University Press, 1987), 207–17.

121. Marcus J. Borg, *Jesus: A New Vision: Spirit, Culture, and the Life of Discipleship* (San Francisco: Harper & Row, 1987).

122. My term, obviously derived from reading Mary Douglas (see n. 156).

123. Borg, *Jesus*, 190.

124. Dwight Moody Smith, "A Review of Marcus J. Borg, Jesus: A New Vision," *Forum* 5, no. 4 (1990): 71–82; the quotation is on 78.

125. While Brandon's reconstruction of the historical Jesus

has been abandoned by scholars, he did urge us (and I think rightly) to begin with studying Jesus from the end and attempting to comprehend why the Romans crucified him. See Brandon, "Further Quest for the Historical Jesus," *Modern Churchman* 5 (1961): 212–20.

126. Borg, *Jesus,* endnote on 168.

127. Hans Conzelmann, *Jesus* (Philadelphia: Fortress, 1973).

128. Barnabas Lindars, *Jesus: Son of Man: A Fresh Examination of the Son of Man Sayings in the Gospels in the Light of Recent Research* (Grand Rapids: Eerdmans, 1983).

129. A. J. B. Higgins, *Jesus and the Son of Man* (London: Lutterworth, 1964). Chrys C. Carogounis, *The Son of Man,* Wissenschaftliche Untersuchungen zum Neuen Testament 38 (Tübingen, 1986).

130. D. R. A. Hare, *The Son of Man Tradition* (Minneapolis: Augsburg Fortress, 1990).

131. Hare, *The Son of Man Tradition,* 278–80.

132. B. F. Meyer, *The Aims of Jesus* (London, 1979), 221. Also see Meyer, "Jesus Christ," *Anchor Bible Dictionary* (1992), 3:773–96. Meyer correctly affirms that "Jesus...was indeed the founder of Christianity" (795).

133. Odo Camponovo, *Königtum, Königsherrschaft und Reich Gottes in den Frühjüdischen Schriften,* Orbis Biblicus et Orientalis 58 (Göttingen: Vandenhoeck & Ruprecht, 1984).

134. Helmut Merklein, *Jesu Botschaft von der Gottesherrschaft,* 3d ed., Stuttgarter Bibelstudien 111 (Stuttgart: Verlag Katholisches Bibelwerk, 1989).

135. Martin Hengel and A. M. Schwemer, eds., *Königsherrschaft Gottes und himmlischer Kult im Judentum, Urchristentum und in der hellenistischen Welt,* Wissenschaftliche Untersuchungen zum Neuen Testament 55 (Tübingen, 1991). See especially the chapter on Jesus' teaching and the Rule of God by H. Merkel.

136. Brad H. Young correctly examines Jesus' parables in light of rabbinic parables; he concludes that Jesus' use of God's Rule denoted not an impending eschatological catastrophe, but a present reality. See Young, *Jesus and His Jewish Parables* (New York: Paulist Press, 1989).

137. See the publications of the Princeton Dead Sea Scrolls Project; these books are published by J. C. B. Mohr (Paul Siebeck) and Westminster/John Knox.

138. Borg, *Jesus,* 184.

139. Martin Buber, *Two Types of Faith* (New York, 1952), 12–13; see also Borg, *Jesus,* 184.

140. Borg, *Jesus,* 180.

141. Joachim Jeremias, *Unknown Sayings of Jesus* (London: S.P.C.K., 1964); F. F. Bruce, *Jesus and Christian Origins outside the New Testament* (London: Hodder & Stoughton, 1974); David Wenham, ed., *The Jesus Tradition outside the Gospels* (Sheffield: JSOT Press, 1985); William D. Stroker, *Extra-canonical Sayings of Jesus* (Atlanta: Scholars Press, 1988). Helmut Koester, *Ancient Christian Gospels* (Philadelphia: Trinity Press International, 1990). Also see Otfried Hofius, "Unknown Sayings of Jesus," in *The Gospel and the Gospels,* ed. Peter Stuhlmacher, trans. J. S. Bowden (Grand Rapids: W. B. Eerdmans, 1991). For a helpful assessment of the New Testament Apocrypha and Pseudepigrapha for Jesus Research see Craig A. Evans, "Jesus in Noncanonical Historical Sources, in *Jesus,* 113–35.

142. James H. Charlesworth, *The New Testament Apocrypha and Pseudepigrapha: A Guide to Publications, with Excursuses on Apocalypses,* ATLA Bibliography Series 17 (Metuchen, N.J.: Scarecrow, 1987).

143. John Dominic Crossan, *Four Other Gospels: Shadows on the Contours of Canon* (Minneapolis: Winston Press, 1985).

144. Also see John Dominic Crossan, *The Historical Jesus: The Life of a Mediterranean Jewish Peasant* (San Francisco: Harper San Francisco, 1992). Crossan paints the portrait of Jesus as a Galilean peasant who was a social revolutionary and compassionate healer. See the reactions to the study of the apocryphal documents for Jesus Research by Raymond E. Brown, "The Gospel of Thomas and St. John's Gospel," *New Testament Studies* 9 (1963): 155–77. See the rejection of the apocryphal works in the study of the historical Jesus by John P. Meier, in *A Marginal Jew.*

145. Smith, "The Problem of John and the Synoptics in Light of the Relation between Apocryphal and Canonical Gospels," in *John and the Synoptics,* ed. Adelbert Denaux, Bibliotheca Ephemeridum Theologicarum Lovaniensium 101 (Leuven: University Press, 1992), 147–62.

146. Wilhelm Schneemelcher, ed., *New Testament Apocrypha,* ed. and trans. R. M. Wilson, 2 vols. (Louisville: Westminster/John Knox, 1991–92).

147. Hengel, *The Charismatic Leader.* Also see P. Hoffman, *Das Erbe Jesu und die Macht in der Kirche,* Topos 213 (Mainz, 1991), especially 16–19, 42–44.

148. Theissen, *Sociology of Early Palestinian Christianity;* in addition to Horsley's works cited earlier, see his chapter in the present book.

149. Douglas E. Oakman, *Jesus and the Economic Questions of His Day* (Lewiston, N.Y.: Edwin Mellen, 1986).

150. Horsley, *Sociology and the Jesus Movement*, 127–28.

151. The most important works for Jesus Research by Max Weber and Emile Durkheim are the following: Weber, H. H. Gerth, and C. Wright Mills, *From Max Weber: Essays in Sociology* (New York: Oxford University Press, 1946, 1958); Weber, *The Theory of Social and Economic Organization*, trans. A. M. Henderson and Talcott Parsons (New York, London, 1947, 1964); Weber, *The Sociology of Religion*, trans. Ephraim Fischoff (Boston, 1963); Durkheim, *The Elementary Forms of the Religious Life*, trans. J. W. Swain (New York, 1915); Durkheim, *Moral Education: A Study in the Theory and Application of the Sociology of Education*, trans. E. K. Wilson and H. Schnurer (New York, London, 1961, 1973).

152. Bengt Holmberg, *Sociology and the New Testament: An appraisal* (Minneapolis: Augsburg Fortress, 1990).

153. Jacob Neusner, *Judaism in the Beginning of Christianity* (Philadelphia: Fortress, 1984), 32.

154. Horsley, *Sociology and the Jesus Movement*, 98.

155. J. H. Charlesworth, ed., *The Messiah: Developments in Earliest Judaism and Christianity*, First Princeton Symposium on Judaism and Christian Origins (Minneapolis: Fortress, 1992). The volume contains twenty-five studies by Jewish and Christian specialists.

156. Mary Douglas, *Purity and Danger* (London: Routledge & Kegan Paul, 1966).

157. Victor Turner, *Process, Performance and Pilgrimage: A Study in Comparative Symbology*, Ranchi Anthropology Series 1 (New Delhi, 1979).

158. Victor Turner, "Pilgrimages as Social Processes," *Dramas, Fields, and Metaphors: Symbolic Action in Human Society* (Ithaca, N.Y.: Cornell University Press, 1974), 166–230.

159. Maurice Merleau-Ponty, *Phenomenology of Perception*, trans. Colin Smith (New York: Routledge, 1962), 67–68: "It is necessary to put the surroundings in abeyance the better to see the object, and to lose in background what one gains in focal figure.... Objects form a system in which one cannot show itself without concealing others."

160. Ernst Käsemann, "The Problem of the Historical Jesus," in *Essays on New Testament Themes*, trans. W. J. Montague, Studies in Biblical Theology 41 (London: SCM Press, 1964), 15–47.

161. Ernst Käsemann, *Der Ruf der Freiheit* (Tübingen: J. C.B Mohr [Paul Siebeck], 1972, 1981 [5th ed.]). The quotation is from the English translation: *Jesus Means Freedom*, trans. Frank Clarke (London, 1969; Philadelphia: Fortress Press, 1970), 19.

162. Nils Dahl, *Jesus in the Memory of the Early Church* (Minneapolis: Augsburg, 1976), 29.

163. See the list of their publications in Evans, *Life of Jesus Research.*

164. See especially, Priscilla Pope-Levison and John R. Levison, *Jesus in Global Contexts* (Louisville: Westminster/John Knox, 1992).

165. Jaroslav Pelikan, *Jesus through the Centuries: His Place in the History of Culture* (New Haven: Yale University Press, 1985), 11.

166. Edward Schillebeeckx, *Jesus: An Experiment in Christology,* trans. H. Hoskins (New York: Crossroad, 1979), 82.

167. Paula Fredriksen, *From Jesus to Christ: The Origins of the New Testament Images of Jesus* (New Haven: Yale University Press, 1988), 214.

168. See some related reflections in the first volume in the present series of books: James H. Charlesworth and Walter P. Weaver, eds., *What Has Archaeology to Do with Faith?* Faith and Scholarship Colloquies 1 (Philadelphia: Trinity Press International, 1992).

169. This heading was on the cover of *Macleans* (Canada's weekly newsmagazine) of December 21, 1992 (note the date, just before Christmas). Barbara Thiering is the proponent of the maverick hypothesis that Jesus lived until the age of seventy. Her views are found in *Jesus and the Riddle of the Dead Sea Scrolls* (San Francisco: Harper San Francisco, 1992). Another extreme and clearly unscholarly approach, also published in 1992, is found in Gore Vidal's *Live from Golgotha* (New York: Random House).

Such books are not to be confused with the scholarly contributions to Jesus Research reviewed above. An assessment of the contributions by Sanders, Mack, Schüssler Fiorenza, and Horsley was published by Borg (and came to my attention when this essay had already been sent to the publisher. See Borg, "Portraits of Jesus in Contemporary North American Scholarship," *Harvard Theological Review* 84 (1991): 1–22.

Chapter 2

Jesus and Eschatology: A Reassessment

Marcus J. Borg

Before I introduce my topic, I want to say something very briefly about the academic discipline in which it is located, namely, historical Jesus scholarship. It is an exciting time for those of us involved in historical Jesus Research, one of those periods when a long-established discipline is undergoing a significant renewal. After a period of relative lack of interest in the historical Jesus, which dominated most of this century, the decade of the 1980s has seen a burst of interest and scholarly activity around the question, What was Jesus like as a figure of history before his death?

James Charlesworth of Princeton has called attention to the birth of a new era in Jesus scholarship with the provocative statement, "Jesus Research commenced around 1980,"[1] N. Thomas Wright of Oxford has spoken of a "third quest" for the historical Jesus now underway,[2] and I have spoken of a "renaissance in Jesus scholarship."[3] Indeed, it may not be going too far to see the present as a time of the greatest ferment and fruitfulness in Jesus scholarship since the time of Schweitzer at the beginning of this century. A major element in that renaissance is a thorough-going questioning of the eschatological consensus that has dominated much of this century's Jesus scholarship. And that is my topic: "Jesus and Eschatology: A Reassessment." My central claim is that the dominant eschatological consensus has seriously eroded. Indeed, as a consensus it has collapsed. In its place are emerging new understandings of Jesus and his message that not only are reshaping the scholarly paradigm, but also have significance for the life of the church. I will develop that claim under four headings: (1) a brief description of the old consensus; (2) the erosion of that consensus; (3) how Jesus and eschatology are seen in six contemporary North American portraits of Jesus; (4) a clarification of my own understanding. Finally, I will conclude with some brief observations about implications for scholarship and the life of the church.

THE OLDER ESCHATOLOGICAL VIEW AND ITS DOMINANCE

The view that dominated twentieth-century Jesus scholarship until recently originated near the beginning of the century in the work of Johannes Weiss and Albert Schweitzer.[4] Their work brought the nineteenth-century quest for the historical Jesus (now commonly known as "the old quest" or "first quest") to a close. The "old quest" was marked by the "liberal lives of Jesus," which portrayed Jesus primarily as a teacher of timeless religious and moral truths.[5] Weiss and Schweitzer radically challenged this position. For both, their central claim was that eschatology was the key to understanding the historical Jesus. Put most simply, they claimed that the most central conviction of Jesus' life — the foundation of his self-understanding, mission, and message — was eschatological. By this they meant that Jesus expected "the end of the world" in his own generation, understood as involving the end-time events of resurrection, last judgment, and the coming of the new and messianic age. All of this (it hardly needs to be said) would involve a radical change in life as we know it, brought about by direct divine intervention ("the Kingdom of God erupting dynamically from above," to use James Charlesworth's useful phrase for describing the "supernatural" coming of the Kingdom).[6] For both, this is what Jesus meant by the coming of the Kingdom of God.

This expectation was found especially in two groups of sayings: sayings that speak of the coming of the Kingdom of God in the near future; and sayings that speak of the coming of "the Son of Man." That Jesus expected the imminent end of the world was also seen as the best explanation of the early church's eschatological expectation: Paul, the authors of Matthew and Mark, the John who authored Revelation, and others in the early church spoke of the second coming of Christ as an eschatological event expected in the near future. Where did they get this notion? From Jesus' own message about the nearness of the Kingdom of God and the coming of the Son of Man. In short, Jesus was an eschatological figure with an eschatological mission and message.

This understanding became the dominant or consensus understanding of Jesus during those periods of Jesus scholarship now called the time of "no quest" and "new quest" (or "second quest"), a span of time stretching from around 1920 to 1970. Two features marked this fifty-year period: we cannot know much about Jesus, and what we can know is that he was an eschatological prophet. To be sure, within this consensus understanding, there was disagreement about some matters. For example, was Jesus' self-understanding messianic or nonmessianic? Did he think of himself as the "coming Son of Man" who would soon return as judge, or did he refer to someone else as "the coming Son of Man"? Did he speak of the Kingdom as only future, or also as present? But there was agreement about the central claim: Jesus' mission and message were permeated by the conviction that his generation lived in "the end of time."

This consensus commonly generated three consequences. First, as is well known, it led to a growing sense of the theological irrelevance of the historical Jesus. Second, it produced a widespread individualized and internalized understanding of the message of Jesus. We can see this especially in the work and influence of Rudolf Bultmann (1884–1976), the "giant" of New Testament scholarship in the middle third of this century. Bultmann affirmed the eschatological understanding argued by Weiss and Schweitzer and made it central to his program of demythologizing and existentialist interpretation. Jesus' expectation of the imminent coming of the Kingdom of God was reinterpreted to mean the imminent end of the world *for the individual*. In every hour, individuals are called by the message of Jesus to ground their existence (their identity and security) in God and not in the world; for those who do so, the world has passed away. Thus every hour is (potentially) the last hour. Through existentialist interpretation, the eschatology of Jesus is radically internalized and individualized, even though the claim that Jesus himself apparently expected an external and objective end in the near future remained.

The third consequence was an apolitical reading of the message and activity of Jesus. The logic is simple: if the end of the world is near, do historical and political questions and institutions matter? Schweitzer gave the obvious answer in his comment on the question of paying taxes to Caesar: "How could one be concerned at all about such things? What need had one to decide if one would be tributary to the world-power or no? One might as well submit to it, its end was in fact near."[7] The eschatological elimination or relativization of historical, social and political questions has become a *leitmotif* of Jesus scholarship that continues into the present, even though (as we shall see later), a sociopolitical reading of eschatology has recently emerged.[8]

Although British New Testament scholarship tended to resist the eschatological consensus, the view that Jesus was an "end-of-the-world" figure dominated German New Testament scholarship and much of North American scholarship through the middle third of this century. Its influence can be seen not only in New Testament scholarship, but in the work of other religious scholars who are dependent on New Testament scholarship for their description of Jesus and the early Christian movement. Most introductory texts to the world's religions routinely present Jesus as an "end-of-the-world" figure and early Christianity as an "end-of-the-world" movement.

THE EROSION OF THE CONSENSUS

It is this consensus that has eroded. Indeed, as a consensus it no longer exists. The evidence that it is no longer shared by a majority of Jesus scholars is considerable. Polls taken of two groups of Jesus scholars in the mid-1980s disclosed that 60 percent of them do not think that Jesus expected the end of the world in his generation.[9] Claremont's James Robinson, one of the best-known North American senior New Testament scholars, has recently spoken of "a Copernican revolution" and "a paradigm shift in the field," which he describes as "the fading of apocalyptic" and the replacement of an eschatological image of Jesus with a sapiential (wisdom) understanding.[10] And, as we shall see in our survey of recent North American portraits of Jesus, five of six no longer see Jesus as an "end the world figure" in the sense affirmed by the former consensus.

It is illuminating to note the factors contributing to the erosion of the consensus. Five seem particularly important.

The first is a change in our understanding of the "coming Son of Man" sayings.[11] Beginning in the 1960s, these increasingly began to be seen not as authentic to Jesus, but as post-Easter creations expressing the early Christian movement's developing belief in the second coming: Jesus would come again "on clouds" as the Son of Man, as either (or both) advocate or judge.

Norman Perrin's 1967 book *Rediscovering the Teaching of Jesus* was perhaps most responsible for bringing this understanding of the "coming Son of Man" sayings into the mainstream of North American scholarship.[12] Though some scholars still argue for the authenticity to Jesus of language about a coming Son of Man, most do not.[13] The change in the scholarly assessment of these texts had an initially unnoticed implication: if they are not authentic, then the textual basis for affirming that Jesus expected the imminent end of the world virtually disappears. The "coming Son of Man" texts are the central underpinning of the image of Jesus as eschatological prophet. Without them, what texts would one point to as a basis for saying that Jesus expected the imminent end and judgment of the world?

The second factor is a more refined understanding of Jewish apocalyptic literature. "Apocalyptic" and "end of the world" have virtually been identified in the world of scholarship. The results of a study group operating within the Society of Biblical Literature during the 1970s point to a different picture. That group studied fifteen Jewish apocalypses and put them into two main categories. The first category is "visionary-historical," that is, visions that speak about a coming end of the world. This category is most familiar to most people because the two primary canonical apocalypses (the second half of Daniel, and the book of Revelation) are both examples of it.

The second category is "visionary other-worldly journey" apocalypses, that is, works that report what the "seer" has seen as a result of a shamanic-like journey into "the other world" and that do not concern a coming end within or at the end of history. Strikingly, of the fifteen apocalypses studied, the majority (eight) are of this second type; six are of the first type, and one has characteristics of both.[14] The point: even apocalyptic language does not necessarily point to an "end-of-the-world" focus. In some instances, it has more in common with Jewish mysticism.

The third factor is the "picture" or "profile" of Jesus
that has emerged from the study of the wisdom forms of
his teaching and from the growing consensus that these
wisdom forms are the earliest layer of the Jesus tradition.[15] Not only are the parables and aphorisms seen as
the "bedrock" of the Jesus tradition, but their function
as subversive and invitational forms of speech point to
an image of Jesus quite different from a preacher of repentance who expected the imminent end of the world.
Indeed, it is difficult to believe that the same person who
told world-subverting stories and spoke subversive aphorisms could also have been dominated by the conviction
that the end of the world and the last judgment were literally at hand. It is perhaps not impossible to affirm both,
but the two are an awkward combination, so awkward as
to seem to me improbable.

The fourth factor is a growing awareness of how much
Mark's Gospel has contributed to the scholarly understanding of the centrality and imminence of the Kingdom
of God in the message of Jesus. It is Mark who says that
the "nearness" or "at handness" of the Kingdom of God
was the heart of Jesus' message. Such is the impression created by Jesus' first words in Mark, the "inaugural address"
that functions as Mark's advance summary of the message
of Jesus: "The time is fulfilled, and the Kingdom of God
is at hand, repent" (Mark 1:15). Though scholars routinely
recognize that this verse is redactional, it is also common
for them to treat the verse as if it were an accurate crystal-
lization of Jesus' message. Yet one wonders. If we did not
have Mark 1:15, would we identify the Kingdom of God
as *the* central theme of Jesus' message? We would see it as
a central image, yes; but as *the* central theme? Moreover,
it is Mark who has most contributed to an understanding
of the Kingdom of God as involving the end of the world.
This understanding of the Kingdom is the most plausible
way of reading Mark 9:1: "Truly I tell you, there are some
standing here who will not taste death until they see the
Kingdom of God come with power." An earlier generation

of critics was virtually unanimous in seeing this verse as authentic and as pointing to imminent end-of-the-world eschatology. More recent scholarship (again represented by Norman Perrin's 1967 book) tends to see this verse as inauthentic. Indeed, Mark 9:1, 1:15, and "the little apocalypse" of Mark 13, climaxing in "the Son of Man coming in clouds with great power and glory" to gather the elect before that generation would pass away (13:24–30), seem to be "all of a piece" and reflective of Mark's theology. Taken together, they suggest that Mark, written around 70 C.E., is an "end-of-the-world" Gospel. But rather than accurately representing Jesus as announcing the end of the world, it may well be that Mark reflects an intense expectation of the end of the world provoked by the events of 66–70 C.E. (the great war with Rome, culminating in the destruction of Jerusalem and the Temple). That is, the picture we get of the centrality and imminence of the Kingdom of God in Mark (including Mark 1:15) is the product of Mark's redaction during a time of intensified eschatological expectation.

The suggestion that the imminent eschatology of Mark belongs to the developmental (or even compositional) layer of the Gospel tradition rather than to an original layer affects our understanding of the role of end-of-the-world expectation in the early Christian movement, as reflected in the synoptic Gospels. Matthew basically takes over Mark's eschatological expectation. Thus, like Mark, Matthew continues to expect the imminent second coming of Christ. Luke has a quite different picture; there is little material in Luke suggesting an imminent parousia. Within the framework of the formerly dominant paradigm, Mark and Matthew were seen as continuing the emphasis of Jesus, and Luke was understood as accommodating the tradition to the delay of the parousia. But what if it's the other way around? That is, what if Matthew and Mark represent an intensification of eschatological expectation rather than Luke representing a diminishment? If this is the case, then the author of Luke, though writing later than Mark and perhaps "correcting" the imminent eschatology of Mark,

actually represents an earlier (and more historically authentic) understanding of Jesus' Kingdom language. That
there was such an earlier non–end-of-the-world understanding of Jesus' Kingdom language is also suggested by
the previously mentioned recent work on Q and Thomas.[16]

The fifth and last factor is a growing tendency among
scholars to see Jesus' relationship to his social world as central to his activity and message and not just as background.
Recent scholarship (as we shall see below) has increasingly
called attention to Jesus' concern with the transformation
of central features of his social world, a concern that ill ac-
cords with the conviction that the world of history and
society was soon to end.

ESCHATOLOGY IN RECENT NORTH AMERICAN "PROFILES" OF JESUS

Taken together, these factors not only contributed to the
erosion of the eschatological consensus, but have also led to
new sketches or construals or profiles of the historical Jesus
quite different from the image of him as an eschatological prophet. Six recent relatively comprehensive sketches
or "profiles" of Jesus, all published by scholars in North
America in the last ten years, illustrate both the collapse
of the old consensus as a consensus and different ways in
which the relationship between Jesus and eschatology is
seen.[17]

Among these, only Ed Sanders's construal of Jesus
continues to see Jesus within the framework of the formerly dominant paradigm. In his 1985 book *Jesus and
Judaism*, Sanders argues that Jesus was a deeply Jewish figure standing in a particular stream or strand of Judaism,
namely, the tradition of Jewish restoration eschatology.[18]
According to Sanders, Jesus believed that the eschatological restoration of Israel and the coming of the messianic
age were at hand. This would involve a number of quite
specific and "concrete" events: the Temple would be de-

stroyed and replaced by a new Temple. Jerusalem would be the center of the messianic age, and Jesus and his disciples would rule over a restored Israel. Though some of the details differ from Schweitzer's portrait at the beginning of this century, imminent eschatology remains and is central. Jesus expected all of this soon, to be brought about by divine intervention; and, of course, like Schweitzer's Jesus, Sanders's Jesus was deeply mistaken.[19]

Burton Mack's sketch of Jesus is the polar opposite of Sanders's.[20] For Mack, Jesus is neither eschatological nor very Jewish. Put positively, Mack sees Jesus as a Cynic-like sage, more similar to Hellenistic Cynic sages than to traditional Jewish types of religious figures. The basis for this construal of Jesus is Mack's analysis of the Gospel traditions, most of which are attributed to the creativity of various Jesus groups and Christ movements in the decades after Easter (Mack's position is the most "minimalist" of the six we shall survey). The earliest layer consists of a portion of the parables and aphorisms. These express a world-mocking wisdom marked by "aphoristic speech, a touch of humor, a critical stance," and "a dare to be different if not outrageous."[21] Jesus was a gadfly, a scoffer and mocker who engaged in a general and often playful ridicule of the preoccupations that animated and imprisoned people. He was not concerned with Jewish traditions or institutions; such concern was simply part of the preoccupation with the world that he rejected. With regard to eschatology, Mack completely eliminates it from his sketch of Jesus. Such texts, with their threats of judgment, are the product of the Jesus movement as it began to encounter opposition and rejection in the decades after the death of Jesus.

The next two portraits — by Richard Horsley and Elisabeth Schüssler Fiorenza — occupy a middle ground between Sanders's imminent eschatology and Mack's elimination of eschatology.

Using studies of peasant societies as his framework, Horsley, the most prolific of contemporary North

American Jesus scholars, sets the traditions about Jesus in the context of a social world whose central dynamic was the conflict between ruling elites and the vast peasant majority.[22] In this setting, Jesus' words and actions disclose that he was a radical social prophet who sought to bring about a social revolution in the life of local communities. Jesus radically criticized the ruling elites (both Jewish and Roman) and called his peasant hearers to a radical reorganization of village life into communities of solidarity. More than any other mainstream scholar (though consistent with Schüssler Fiorenza and my own work), Horsley offers a sociopolitical reading of the Jesus tradition.

Horsley thoroughly integrates eschatology into his portrait of Jesus as a social revolutionary. He does so in two ways. First, he argues that many apocalyptic texts have a historical orientation and gives them a sociopolitical reading. Commonly arising out of conditions of oppression, such texts have three functions: the remembering of past acts of divine deliverance, the creative envisioning of a radically different and better future, and the critical demystifying of the established order by stripping the ruling class of divine authority and exposing its demonic character. Thus, for him, apocalyptic texts express "in ordinary contemporary language eager hopes for an anti-imperial revolution" to be brought about by God.[23] They do not have an "other-worldly" or "next-worldly" orientation, but express hope for a this-worldly transformation.

Second, Horsley argues for a primarily "this-worldly" understanding of the Kingdom of God. Speaking of it as a "political metaphor," he sees it as referring to something happening even then, a historical transformation already underway, a "society" of people already coming into existence. The Kingdom meant wholeness of life in a community marked by "a new spirit of cooperation and mutual assistance."[24]

At only one point does a trace of imminent "Kingdom erupting dynamically from above" eschatology remain. Horsley assimilates it by making a distinction between *social revolution* and *political revolution;* the former is a "bottom-up" revolution, the latter a "top-down" revolution. Jesus began the former and expected God soon to initiate the latter: "God would soon judge the oppressive imperial regime."[25] Thus, for Horsley, imminent end-of-the-world language in the message of Jesus refers to a coming dramatic change in political control, to be accomplished directly by God. Yet imminent end-of-the-world eschatology, in its usual sense, is not central for Horsley. It plays no fundamental foundational role in his construal of Jesus. It is neither the foundation of Jesus' self-understanding, as it was for Schweitzer and as it is for Sanders, nor the animating motive behind Jesus' mission, nor the primary content of Jesus' message. Rather, it is integrated into a picture of Jesus as a social prophet passionately engaged in shaping his social world. It is a "this-worldly" and "transformist" understanding of eschatology.[26]

Such is also the case for Elisabeth Schüssler Fiorenza, arguably the most important and influential feminist New Testament scholar. In her 1983 book *In Memory of Her,* she sketches a picture of the Jesus movement as a renewal movement within Israel.[27] Though she eschews any attempt to understand Jesus apart from the movement that he brought into existence, some clear strokes of a portrait of Jesus emerge. As a figure of history, Jesus was a "wisdom prophet," by which she means two things. On the one hand, Jesus was a *prophet of wisdom,* that is, a prophet or spokesperson for divine Sophia. On the other hand, he was a wisdom prophet in the sense of being a social prophet who called into existence an egalitarian movement that affirmed a vision of human life in community very different from the dominant ethos of his time. The embodiment of this vision in "a discipleship of equals" sharply challenged his social world's preoccupation with purity and patriarchy.

Like Horsley, she integrates eschatology into her image of Jesus as a socially radical wisdom prophet and

movement founder. Though affirming a form of the dominant consensus (Kingdom as both future and present, as
both eschatological vision and experiential reality), she almost completely emphasizes the present. In Jesus' ministry,
"eschatological salvation and wholeness" were "already
experientially available."[28] The coming of the Kingdom
had an already present social impact: Jesus' "praxis and vision of the *basileia* is the mediation of God's future into the
structures and experiences of his own time and people."[29]
Though she acknowledges that Jesus' *basileia* language
also referred to a future in which death and suffering
would be no more, this expectation plays no significant
role in her image of Jesus and his movement. Rather, Jesus
was concerned with a "this-worldly" transformation of
his society's life. Jesus' language about the Kingdom did
not point primarily to a future reversal, but to a reversal
that was already happening. Thus, like Horsley, Schüssler
Fiorenza affirms a transformist eschatology.

   The fifth sketch I will report is of John Dominic
Crossan. For the past two decades, Crossan has been
known especially for his work on the wisdom forms
(parables and aphorisms) of Jesus' teaching.[30] His very
recent comprehensive treatment of Jesus *(The Historical
Jesus: The Life of a Mediterranean Jewish Peasant)* may be
the most significant scholarly book about Jesus published
in several decades. It is remarkable for two things in addition to its construal of Jesus. First, more than any other
scholar, Crossan has developed a systematic methodology for "layering" the Jesus tradition into various strata,
and his method is likely to be the subject of discussion for
many years. Second, more than any other single volume,
Crossan's book incorporates a multidisciplinary approach,
regularly providing summary accounts of works in other
fields that illuminate the dynamics and phenomena of
Jesus' social world and of the Gospel texts themselves.

   In this book, Crossan fills out his earlier sketch of Jesus
as a teacher of a world-subverting and world-shattering
wisdom by adding two further major strokes: Jesus as

healer (Crossan's preferred term is "magician"), and Jesus as one who practiced "open commensality" (eating with others without regard to social boundaries). Both point to a "social" dimension of Jesus' activity and to a radically egalitarian vision. The key to the "social reading" of Jesus as healer is found in Crossan's use of the word "magician," which he does not use in a pejorative sense, but in the sense of "religious banditry": one who offers healing outside of institutionally sanctioned religious authority. "Open commensality" (or open "table fellowship," to use a phrase from earlier scholarship), in the context of his social world, was a strategy for building or rebuilding peasant community on principles radically different from the ethos of that social world. Taken together, "free healing and common eating" embodied "a religious and economic egalitarianism that negated alike and at once the hierarchical and patronal normalcies of Jewish religion and Roman power."[31]

His treatment of eschatology reflects the collapse of the old consensus. He denies imminent end-of-the-world eschatology to Jesus (which he calls "apocalyptic eschatology") and argues that the coming Son of Man sayings are the product of the early church. Rather than an "apocalyptic Kingdom of God," he sees Jesus affirming a "sapiential Kingdom," a "kingdom of nobodies" and "undesirables," "here and now." Neither "apocalyptic eschatology" nor "Kingdom as future" was part of the message of Jesus.

Finally, I wish to conclude this section by briefly describing my own construal of Jesus.[32] There are four broad strokes in my sketch. First, Jesus was a "Spirit person" (or, to use the older noninclusive term, a "holy man") in the charismatic stream of Judaism. As one experientially in touch with what his tradition spoke of as "the Spirit," he was a "mediator of the Spirit," not only as a healer but as a teacher "who spoke with authority," i.e., "from the mouth of the Gevurah."[33] The second stroke in my sketch is a wisdom stroke: he was an unconventional "wisdom teacher" who taught a subversive wisdom that was also an alternative wisdom. The third stroke calls attention to his involvement in the world of history and politics: he was a social prophet who radically challenged the dominant political paradigm of his social world ("purity," which could also be spoken of as "holiness"), criticized ruling elites, and warned them of the disastrous consequences facing them if they did not change. Fourth and finally, I also see Jesus as a "movement founder," who called into existence a Jewish revitalization movement whose purpose was to embody the alternative vision that animated him.

Regarding eschatology, I have consistently denied that Jesus proclaimed an "imminent end-of-the-world" eschatology (in the sense used by Weiss, Schweitzer, Bultmann, etc.). Negatively, I argue that the foundation of the former consensus — "the coming Son of Man" sayings — has largely disappeared; rather than being authentic to Jesus, they are better understood as "second coming" texts produced within the early movement. Positively, I argue that the conflict traditions in the Gospels, when set within the framework of the politico-religious dynamics of the Jewish social world, disclose that Jesus was concerned with the "shaping" of this world. Finally, I argue that the strong tone of crisis in his message does not derive from expectation of the eschaton, but points to sociohistorical crisis. The conflict and crisis traditions are best understood using the model of the classical prophets of ancient Israel, not the model of a preacher of the imminent end of the world.

These six portraits of Jesus fairly represent the range and diversity of recent mainstream North American Jesus scholarship. They suggest, as I indicated at the beginning, that the eschatological consensus is no more. Of the six, only one (Sanders) affirms a version of the old consensus. Of the rest, three (Mack, Crossan, my own) explicitly deny to Jesus an imminent end-of-the-world eschatology ("Kingdom as erupting dynamically from above," and *soon*). Two (Horsley and Schüssler Fiorenza) contain a "nod" in the direction of the old consensus, but then radically relativize "Kingdom erupting dynamically from above in the near future," subsuming it to an emphasis upon a socially transformist eschatology already at work.

Thus five of these six portraits depart significantly from the profile or image of Jesus that dominated scholarly thinking about Jesus and Christian origins throughout much of this century. That image — of Jesus as an eschatological prophet who mistakenly proclaimed the imminent end of the world — is being replaced by quite different images. Noteworthy also is the growing tendency to affirm that Jesus was concerned with the "shape" of this world, rather than announcing its end. Four of these six portraits (all but Sanders and Mack) see the Jesus tradition as containing a vision of social transformation. The "eschatological exclusion of politics" that has dominated much of this century's scholarship is clearly on the wane. To a considerable extent, the image of Jesus as eschatological prophet is being replaced with an image of Jesus as a wisdom figure and a social prophet.

CLARIFYING THE ESCHATOLOGICAL DISCUSSION

The debate about an eschatological or noneschatological understanding of the teaching and activity of Jesus suffers greatly from terminological confusion. In this century's scholarship, "eschatology" has come to have such a wide range of meanings that it is difficult to know what is being affirmed (or denied) when one ascribes (or denies) imminent eschatological expectation to Jesus.

So far as we know, the term "eschatology" entered theological discourse in the seventeenth century. First used by Abraham Calov in 1677, it was the title of the last section of his dogmatics, in which he treated "the last things." In his case, this involved death and postdeath states, judgment, consummation, hell and everlasting death, and life everlasting.[34] "Eschatology" thus truly meant "last things," including what Christians have usually thought of as the meaning of the phrase "the end of the world."

This is the sense in which Weiss and Schweitzer used the word "eschatology." The coming of the Kingdom of God meant "the last things": divine intervention, resurrection of the dead, last judgment, and the dawning of the messianic age or everlasting Kingdom. Though more temporally conceived than Calov's eschatology, their understanding is still recognizably using the word in the same sense.

Since then it has come to be used in a bewildering number of ways, many of which do not involve the imminent "end of the world" in the sense in which Weiss and Schweitzer meant that. There is the existentialist reading of "end of the world" as a fundamental internal change of the ground of one's security and identity. There is the understanding of eschatology as the "shattering of the (conceptual) world" brought about by the subversive effect of Jesus' parables and aphorisms. It is sometimes used to refer to any "world-shaking" event, so that the tearing down of the Berlin wall can be described as an "eschatological event."[35]

The confusion extends to the word "apocalyptic." At a professional meeting, I heard one scholar say, "Jesus was eschatological, but not apocalyptic." By that he meant, "Jesus spoke of the coming of the Kingdom of God as an eschatological event, but he didn't have a 'roadmap' or 'timetable'" (which implies a certain understanding of apocalyptic). At the same meeting, another scholar said, "Jesus was apocalyptic, but not eschatological." Seemingly, it affirms the opposite of the first statement, but in fact it does not. This scholar understood apocalyptic material as closely connected to Jewish mysticism and not generally with a temporal end of the world. Thus this scholar meant, "Jesus was a Jewish mystic, not an end-of-the-world figure."

Because of the radical ambiguity that "eschatological" has acquired, one scholar has argued that we eliminate it from our vocabulary. I myself have often wondered why the word "eschatological" has continued to be applied to Jesus and his message even when it is used in a sense radically different from what Weiss and Schweitzer meant. My own hunch is that scholars have come to assume that there is an "end-of-the-world" emphasis in the message of Jesus that requires interpretation, and so new meanings of "eschatology" are introduced. To put that differently: if the word "eschatology" had not come to have such a central place in the scholarly discussion through the influence of Weiss and Schweitzer, would it even occur to somebody to argue for these other meanings of "eschatology"?

John Dominic Crossan's explanation of his reason for continuing to use the term "eschatological" is illustrative. Crossan denies that Jesus was an "apocalyptic" figure in the sense of being concerned with the imminent end of the world. Yet he chooses to retain using the word "eschatological" when speaking about Jesus. He explains that "eschatology" is "the wider and generic term *for world-negation* extending from apocalyptic eschatology . . . through mystical or utopian modes, and on to ascetical, libertarian, or anarchistic possibilities."[36] I agree that all of these are forms of "world-negation"; but why use "eschatology" as a *generic term* for "world-negation"? Why not simply use "world-negation"?

My point is not to engage in a terminological quarrel. Crossan is very clear, defining his terms with care and precision. Moreover, he and I agree that imminent eschatology was not part of the message of Jesus, and I have even used the phrase "mystical eschatology" myself when speaking about Jesus' orientation.[37] My point rather is to illustrate the persistence of the term "eschatology" in our discipline, even when it is being used in a sense radically different from that given to it by Weiss and Schweitzer. Would one use the word "eschatological" for "world-negation" if it were not for the assumption that there is an eschatological emphasis in the message of Jesus that must be interpreted in some way?

However, though a moratorium on the use of the word "eschatology" might be desirable, it is unlikely. What one can insist upon is precision in specifying the sense in which one is using the term when one either affirms or denies "eschatological expectation" to Jesus. When I deny "eschatological expectation" to Jesus, specifically I am denying "imminent end-of-the-world eschatology" to Jesus. I understand "end-of-the-world eschatology" to include the traditional eschatological events of "objective" divine intervention ("the Kingdom of God erupting dynamically from above"), "last judgment," and the beginning of a new age, all occurring in a publicly visible and unmistakable way. It *need not* involve "the end of the earth";[38] in the messianic age, the world of Jerusalem, banquets, and vineyards may remain. But it is an "objective" change of affairs brought about by divine intervention, so dramatic that even outsiders would have to recognize it.[39]

Thus by the word "eschatology" I mean "last things." By "imminent eschatology" I mean the conviction that the "last things" are temporally near. When I deny imminent eschatology to Jesus, I am denying that he expected this kind of divine intervention in the near future. This was not central (or even peripheral) to his message; it is not what he meant by the Kingdom of God.

Having said that, I also think Jesus had an eschatology. Early traditions seem to indicate that he affirmed an afterlife and that he spoke of a last judgment. But neither seems central to his message. Moreover, when he did speak of such matters, he typically countered or subverted popular expectations. A classic example is the debate with the Sadducees reported in Mark 12:18–27. Their question presupposes that the afterlife involves a fairly direct continuation of earthly existence (specifically, the persistence of marriage relationships), and Jesus' response suggests that the afterlife is far different from popular imaginings of it.

Even more interesting are four Q passages (Luke 10:12–15, 11:31–32). In them, Jesus is reported to have spoken of the last judgment and its relationship to the people of his generation: it will be more tolerable on the day of judgment for Sodom, Tyre, and Sidon than for Chorazin, Bethsaida, or Capernaum; the queen of the South and the men of Nineveh "will arise at the judgment with this generation" and condemn it. Two things in particular stand out about these texts. First, they do not say that the judgment is imminent. This is an important point; nothing in these texts says that the judgment is soon. Rather, whenever it comes, long-dead generations (including gentiles) will fare better than some "in this generation." Second, the function of these passages is to reverse or subvert traditional or popular eschatological expectations. It is as if Jesus said, "You think you know what the last judgment will be like? Well, let me tell you what it will be like — the people of Sodom and Nineveh will fare better than many of you."

Thus there is language reflecting a "cosmic eschatology" in Jesus' message. But such texts are not numerous,[40] and when the motif does appear, it challenges rather than affirms conventional eschatological expectations. The subversion of taken-for-granted notions in these last judgment texts is consistent with the image of Jesus as a subversive sage and social prophet. Their purpose is to subvert and indict, and not to proclaim the imminent end of the world.

Finally, it remains to say something about the origin of the early Christian movement's eschatological expectation. The usual way of explaining this is to see it as a continuation of Jesus' own message: he proclaimed the imminent coming of the Kingdom of God, and the early church for the next several decades continued this proclamation in a transformed form. Namely, rather than speaking about the imminent coming of the Kingdom of God, they spoke about the imminent return of Jesus as the Son of Man who would establish and rule that Kingdom.

However, it seems more plausible to locate the origin of the early movement's "end-of-the-world" expectation in the post-Easter situation for two reasons. First, within a

Jewish frame of thought, "resurrection" (as distinct from "resuscitation") was associated with the end of time; if Jesus has been "raised," then the end times must be near. Second, the early church's belief that the end was near was associated with the expectation that Jesus would come again; the "end-of-the-world" texts are "second coming" texts. When did belief in a second coming arise? Presumably only after Easter.

CONCLUSION AND IMPLICATIONS

This completes my case for arguing that imminent end-of-the-world eschatology is not part of the message of Jesus. The reassessment of Jesus and eschatology that has been going on in the discipline for the last decade has a number of interesting implications for both scholarship and the church.

Within the scholarly world, we are already seeing some of the implications. With the old consensus no longer a consensus, the question of what Jesus was like as a figure of history is being answered in fresh ways. If he was not an eschatological preacher of repentance in the face of the coming end, what was he up to? The sketches I have surveyed indicate some of the possibilities. And, contrary to the "apolitical" reading of the Jesus tradition that marked the period of the ascendancy of the old consensus, there is reason to think that a much more sociopolitical reading of the Jesus tradition will characterize the next decade of Jesus scholarship.

This change in scholarship also has implications for the life of the church. Though the question of the theological significance of historical research is a convoluted one, it simply is the case that images of Jesus do affect images of the Christian life. We can see this from the effects of the formerly dominant image of Jesus as an eschatological prophet. For several decades, seminarians learned that we cannot know much about Jesus, and what we can know is that he expected the end of the world and was wrong. The result has been an uncertainty about what to do with the figure and message of Jesus in many mainstream churches. Confident proclamation about Jesus has largely become the property of Christian fundamentalists and others who accept the Gospel accounts at face value.

The emergence of new images of Jesus has the potential for changing this. Though unanimity in a discipline working with problems as difficult as those encountered in Jesus Research will never be achieved, there are some common emphases emerging in the Jesus Research of the past decade. The picture of Jesus as a teacher of a subversive and alternative wisdom and as a figure with an alternative vision of human life in both its individual and communal existence offers rich possibilities for informing the church's understanding of its founder.

NOTES

1. James Charlesworth, "From Barren Mazes to Gentle Rappings: The Emergence of Jesus Research," *Princeton Seminary Bulletin* 7 (1986): 221. See also his *Jesus within Judaism: New Light from Exciting Archaeological Discoveries*, Anchor Bible Reference Library (New York: Doubleday, 1988), in which he highlights this rebirth of Jesus scholarship.

2. N. Thomas Wright and Stephen Neill, *The Interpretation of the New Testament 1861–1986* (New York: Oxford University Press, 1988), 379–403.

3. "A Renaissance in Jesus Studies," *Theology Today* 45 (1988): 280–92.

4. Johannes Weiss, *Jesus' Proclamation of the Kingdom of God*, ed. and trans. R. H. Hiers and D. L. Holland (Philadelphia: Fortress, 1971); first edition published in German in 1892, second edition in 1900. Albert Schweitzer, *The Mystery of the Kingdom of God* (New York: Schocken, 1964), first published in German in 1901; and *The Quest of the Historical Jesus* (New York: Macmillan, 1968), first published in German in 1906 and in English in 1910.

5. For a convenient "mapping" of the quest for the historical Jesus into the periods of "pre-quest," "old quest," "no quest" and "new quest," see W. Barnes Tatum, *In Quest of Jesus* (Atlanta:

John Knox, 1982), 66–79. For the shift in terms to "first quest
(old quest)," "second quest (new quest)," and "third quest,"
see Wright and Neill, *The Interpretation of the New Testament
1861–1986.*

6. I first heard Prof. Charlesworth use this phrase at the
symposium at Florida Southern, where this paper was originally
presented. I do not know if (or where) he may have used it in his
numerous publications.

7. Schweitzer, *The Mystery of the Kingdom of God*, 119

8. Norman Perrin spoke of the "nonpolitical" reading of
the Kingdom of God as established in his 1963 book, *The Kingdom
of God in the Teaching of Jesus*, 20–21 and 21n, 51–52, and credited
it to Weiss and Schweitzer. See also the section "Imminent Eschatology and the Exclusion of Politics" in my *Conflict, Holiness
and Politics in the Teaching of Jesus*, Studies in the Bible and Early
Christianity 5 (Lewiston, N.Y.: Edwin Mellen, 1984), 8–13. The
eschatological exclusion of politics continues into our own time.
See the comment of John P. Meier in his essay, "Reflections on
Jesus-of-History Research Today," in James H. Charlesworth, ed.,
Jesus' Jewishness: Exploring the Place of Jesus within Early Judaism
(New York: Crossroad, 1991), 92: "The historical Jesus seems to
have had no interest in the great political and social questions of
his day. He was not interested in the reform of the world because
he was prophesying its end." For a recent reading of eschatology
that does not exclude but emphatically includes sociopolitical
transformation, see my comments on Richard Horsley and Elisabeth Schüssler Fiorenza later in this essay.

9. Reported in my essay, "A Temperate Case for a Non-
Eschatological Jesus," *Foundations and Facets Forum* 2, no. 3
(1986): 81–102.

10. In a paper he presented at the International Meeting
of the Society of Biblical Literature in August 1990 in Vienna.
Robinson also described the eschatological paradigm as an "old
model which is frayed and blemished, with broken parts, a
Procrustean bed in which the discipline squirms."

11. Exemplary "coming Son of Man" texts include Mark
8:38, 13:24–27, 14:62; Luke 12:8; Matt. 10:23.

12. Norman Perrin, *Rediscovering the Teaching of Jesus* (New
York: Harper & Row, 1967), 164–99.

13. See, for example, the work of "The Jesus Seminar," a
group of scholars which since 1985 has been assessing the degree
to which a scholarly consensus exists on the historical authenticity of the sayings of Jesus. The seminar's voting on the various
"coming Son of Man" sayings has consistently been 80 percent

negative. For the complete results of the seminar's work, see its *The Five Gospels: The Search for the Authentic Words of Jesus*, new translation and commentary by Robert W. Funk, Roy W. Hooren, and the Jesus Seminar; a Polebridge Press Book (New York: Macmillan Publishing Company, 1993). For John Dominic Crossan's thorough and very persuasive case that the coming "Son of Man" sayings are found in a developmental or compositional layer of the tradition rather than in an original layer, see his *The Historical Jesus: The Life of a Mediterranean Jewish Peasant* (San Francisco: Harper San Francisco, 1992), 238–59, especially 243, 254–55.

14. For a readily accessible summary and bibliographic information, see John Collins, *The Apocalyptic Imagination* (New York: Crossroad, 1984), 5–8.

15. Quite apart from how one sees Q and the Gospel of Thomas, it seems clear that the original forms of the parables and aphorisms are in the earliest layer of the Jesus tradition. However, if one takes seriously recent studies of Q that speak of a "layering" of Q (especially, for example, John Kloppenborg, *The Formation of Q* [Philadelphia: Fortress, 1987]), and recent studies of Thomas that find Thomas to contain material as old as anything in the synoptics, then the case becomes even stronger for saying that the earliest layer of the tradition is dominated by wisdom (and not apocalyptic) material.

16. See the previous note.

17. For a more detailed exposition of five of these construals (all but Crossan), see my "Portraits of Jesus in Contemporary North American Scholarship," *Harvard Theological Review* 84 (1991): 1–22.

18. E. P. Sanders, *Jesus and Judaism* (Philadelphia: Fortress, 1985).

19. I might add that I have no problems myself in affirming that Jesus could be mistaken about various things. I take it for granted that he believed many things that we quite properly do not believe (e.g., he probably thought the world was flat, that the universe was relatively small and not very old, that the Torah was written by Moses, etc.). However, the magnitude of the mistake attributed to Jesus by Schweitzer and his successors should be noted: Jesus was mistaken about that which was most central to his message and mission, namely, the imminent expectation of a supernaturally bestowed messianic age ("the Kingdom of God erupting dynamically from above," to use Charlesworth's helpful phrase). Of course, Jesus could have been wrong about this,

too, but the magnitude of this mistake makes it worth arguing about.

20. Burton L. Mack, *A Myth of Innocence: Mark and Christian Origins* (Philadelphia: Fortress, 1988).

21. From a then-unpublished paper sent to me by Prof. Mack in 1990, "Cultural Critique in Antiquity: Diogenes the Cynic and Jesus," 9.

22. For Horsley's most comprehensive treatment, see *Jesus and the Spiral of Violence: Popular Jewish Resistance in Roman Palestine* (San Francisco: Harper & Row, 1987). See also his *Sociology and the Jesus Movement* (New York: Crossroad, 1989), *The Liberation of Christmas: The Infancy Narratives in Social Context* (New York: Crossroad, 1989); and, with John S. Hanson, *Bandits, Prophets and Messiahs: Popular Movements at the Time of Jesus* (Minneapolis: Winston, 1985).

23. Horsley, *Jesus and the Spiral of Violence*, 160.

24. Ibid., 324–25.

25. Ibid., 322.

26. For a sociopolitical "world-transforming" reading of apocalyptic texts similar to that argued by Horsley, see also William R. Herzog, "Apocalypse Then and Now: Apocalyptic and the Historical Jesus Reconsidered," *Pacific Theological Review* 18, no. 1 (Fall 1984), and David Batstone, "Jesus, Apocalyptic and World Transformation," a paper to be presented at the 1992 International Meeting of the Society of Biblical Literature in Melbourne, Australia. I find their claim that apocalyptic texts can be read that way to be persuasive. Where we would differ is not on a sociopolitical reading of the Jesus tradition, but on the question, Are there apocalyptic texts authentic to Jesus that need to be interpreted in some way? And if so, what are they?

27. Elisabeth Schüssler Fiorenza, *In Memory of Her: A Feminist Theological Reconstruction of Christian Origins* (New York: Crossroad, 1983). Most relevant to her sketch of Jesus and the earliest Jesus movement are 72–159.

28. Ibid., 119, 120; see also 111–12, 121.

29. Ibid., 121.

30. See especially *In Parables: The Challenge of the Historical Jesus* (San Francisco: Harper & Row, 1973), and *In Fragments: The Aphorisms of Jesus* (San Francisco: Harper & Row, 1983).

31. Crossan, *The Historical Jesus*, 422. See also 298.

32. My own position is found in embryonic form in my 1972 thesis, "Conflict as a Context for Interpreting the Teaching of Jesus" (Oxford), and in more developed form in two books, *Conflict, Holiness and Politics in the Teachings of Jesus*,

Studies in the Bible and Early Christianity 5 (Lewiston, N.Y.: Edwin Mellen, 1984), and *Jesus: A New Vision* (San Francisco: Harper & Row, 1987). All are marked by a "noneschatological" understanding of Jesus, in the sense that I clarify below.

33. Mark 1:22. On *Gevurah* as referring to the authority or power of God, see Ephraim E. Urbach, *The Sages* (Jerusalem: Magnes, 1975), 80–96, especially 85–86.

34. For the reference to Calov, see the article by Gerhard Sauter, *Scottish Journal of Theology* 41 (1988).

35. In his *The Language and Imagery of the Bible* (London: Duckworth, 1980), George Caird, a persistent critic of the eschatological consensus in the decades when it was still dominant, catalogued seven different senses in which "eschatology" is used, and proposed a subscript system for distinguishing them. See 243–71.

36. Crossan, *The Historical Jesus*, 238; italics added.

37. Borg, *Conflict, Holiness and Politics*, 229, 254–56, 261.

38. In a conversation, Eugene Boring helpfully described *this sense* of "end of the world" as a "molecular" or "nuclear" or "melt-down" eschatology. That is, to say Jesus expected "the end of the world" need not mean that he expected the disappearance of the elements.

39. Crossan's way of stressing the "objective" or "publicly visible" character of this expectation is helpful (*The Historical Jesus*, 238). By "end of the world," he means "a divine intervention so transcendentally obvious that one's adversaries or enemies, oppressors or persecutors would be forced to acknowledge it and to accept conversion or concede defeat." Or, as he put it in a conversation, "An event so obvious that even non-believers would have to say, 'You were right.' "

40. The common impression that there are many such texts is largely due to Matthew's Gospel, arguably the most familiar of the synoptic Gospels. Matthew regularly turns the "threats" of the synoptic tradition into threats of eternal condemnation (such familiar phrases as "being cast into the outer darkness," "weeping and wailing and gnashing of teeth," and the "furnace of fire" are Matthaean), and it is Matthew who sets several of Jesus' parables in the context of "the second coming" and judgment (Matt. 24–25). For an examination of the Matthaean "threat tradition" and a comparison of that to the broader synoptic "threat tradition," see my *Conflict, Holiness and Politics*, 201–21, 266–68.

Chapter 3

Jesus, Itinerant Cynic
or Israelite Prophet?

Richard Horsley

One of the most intriguing ideas that biblical scholars have come up with recently is that Jesus closely resembled a wandering Cynic philosopher. Ironically the idea is one that scholars "stumbled upon" indirectly if not accidentally. Having virtually given up on being able to know much about Jesus himself, many critical students shifted their attention to the first followers of Jesus, or to what some call "the Jesus movement." Only secondarily then did a few especially well acquainted with Hellenistic philosophy suggest that similarities noted between Jesus' first followers and Cynic philosophers should probably be traced back to Jesus himself.

THEISSEN'S WANDERING CHARISMATICS

One might almost read twentieth-century scholarship on Jesus and the synoptic Gospels as driven by two concerns: to respond to the implications of modern scientific reason, and to ward off any political implications of the synoptic Gospel traditions. Most of the narrative material in the Gospels, full of the miraculous, the fantastic, or simply the kerygmatic faith in Christ, was deemed unreliable as historical evidence for Jesus. That also took care of political implications, since most of the indications of social conflict are in the miracle stories, infancy narratives, and passion narratives. Virtually the only materials deemed reliable for investigations into the historical Jesus were the sayings, and the bulk of relevant Jesus' sayings were thought to be contained in "Q," i.e., short for *Quelle*, German for the Source of sayings supposedly used by both Matthew and Luke.

Although he was not the first to articulate it, Gerd Theissen is the most widely read proponent of the notion that these sayings pertained to and were carried by a small number of itinerant followers of Jesus. "Jesus did not primarily found local communities, but called into being a movement of wandering charismatics."[1] According to Theissen's and others' reading, "the ethical radicalism of the sayings tradition" could have been practiced and handed down only "by those who had been released from the everyday ties of the world," that is, by a handful of itinerants in first-century Palestine.[2] He finds three key features in the sayings of Jesus that must have characterized these "wandering charismatics" whom Jesus had called to such a "radical" lifestyle: homelessness, lack of family, and lack of possessions. The principal texts cited repeatedly as evidence for these interrelated features are Mark 1:16, 20 (the calling of disciples); Mark 10:28–29 (leaving house and family for Jesus); Luke 10:4 (take no purse, no bag, etc.); and Luke 14:26. ("hating" father and mother ... ").

Not having found anything comparable in Palestinian Jewish society, Theissen then argued that the ethos of Jesus' sayings is comparable to that of Cynic philosophy in those very three crucial elements: renunciation of home, family, and possessions. He illustrates from Epictetus's famous "Calling of the Cynic":

"How is it possible to live happily without possessions, naked, without house and home, without attention, without a servant, without a country?" and he answers, "Look! God has sent you a person who can prove by his actions that it is possible. I have none of those things. I sleep on the ground. I have no wife, no children, no small palace, but only the earth and sky and a single large coat. And still what do I lack? Am I not free?" (Epictetus, *Dis.* 22:45–48)

Theissen claims that because the Cynic ethos was carried by itinerant philosophers, we can deduce by analogy that those who transmitted the sayings of Jesus belonged to a comparable social group.[3]

Now one does not have to be a sociologist or historian to know that similarities of a few motifs do not necessarily mean similarities in social position and role. And Theissen, of course, does not claim that the wandering charismatics who carried Jesus' sayings were Cynics, just that they were socially analogous. But others suggest that Theissen did not go far enough, that is, to take the next step and suggest that not only were Jesus' itinerant disciples Cynics but that Jesus himself was Cynic-like. Before examining this hypothesis, however, it may be helpful to have a fuller sense of what the Cynics were like.

STRAY DOGS[4]

Cynics were practitioners of one of several types of philosophy stemming from broadly Socratic tradition, having branched off from the Stoics, starting with Diogenes of Sinope. They espoused living according to nature and often flouted social conventions, even to the point of shamelessness. In fact they often displayed a contempt for the masses and ordinary life. "Cynic" means "dog," and the Cynics often behaved like dogs — in public.

Their philosophy was really more a certain lifestyle. Of the three traditional divisions of philosophy, they abandoned physics and logic and concentrated on ethics. They tried to live simply, to endure hardship. A keynote was *self-sufficiency*, hence their *radical individualism*. Their main concern was with how they individually might attain happiness. They gave a great deal of emphasis to *personal decision* to change one's way of living, which means that they defined themselves in opposition to the ordinary people. By relinquishing home and family and possessions, they demonstrated their self-sufficiency and superiority to conventional values. Cynics had a distinctive appearance or dress, featuring particularly a staff and a bag or knapsack. They also went barefoot and, carrying no money, would beg for a living. Begging of course was not disgraceful, because it satisfied nature, a natural need arising from abandoning possessions, which were unnatural.

They also addressed people in public places, challenging social conventions as foolishness and urging others to join their countercultural lifestyle. In this connection some of them honed the art of repartee, having quick witty responses to others, particularly authority figures. Another key trait was thus their *boldness of speech* or *parrēsia*, exemplified in the following anecdote repeated by Diogenes Laertius (6.63): "When a fellow reproached him [Diogenes the Cynic] for going into the privies because they were unclean, he said 'The sun also comes into the privies but is not defiled.' "

Cynicism faded away considerably during the second and first centuries B.C.E., then made a comeback in the late first century C.E., basically as an urban phenomenon.

JESUS AS CYNIC[5]

The argument that Jesus was a Cynic or a Cynic-like figure depends primarily on the similarities of the *style* of some of his teachings in Q to clever Cynic repartee, and it hinges largely around the similarity of some of the motifs in the Q mission discourse to the characteristics of the wandering Cynics, these "stray dogs." Also helpful may be the recognition that the suggestion of a Cynic Jesus has been developed on the assumption of a noneschatological Jesus, the prophetic and apocalyptic sayings having been judged a later accretion to the original collection of Jesus' sayings, which were almost exclusively pithy wisdom teachings.

The sayings in Luke 10:3–11 are the key to the whole argument, particularly 10:4 and 5–6. The sayings about entering houses to eat (10:5–6), are taken as a reference to begging. And 10:4, the saying about what equipment (not) to take on the road — staff, cloak, bag, etc. — is interpreted as an indication of a whole "way of life" of "self-sufficiency and independence" that is distinctively Cynic. The argument, often not completely articulated, is that if Jesus called his disciples to lead such an individual Cynic lifestyle of homeless antifamilial self-sufficiency, then he himself must have been a Cynic as well. When one then adds to this the quick wit and sharp tongue of Jesus in certain sayings such as Luke 9:57–60 ("let the dead bury the dead") or 14:26 ("hate your father and mother"), they are convinced that Jesus' teachings, like the incisive repartee of the Cynics, are basically a countercultural attack on social conventions.

LACK OF TEXTUAL EVIDENCE FOR WANDERING CHARISMATICS OR CYNICS

A glance at the sayings Theissen uses as proof-texts for the existence of the "wandering charismatics" is enough to throw the whole hypothesis into question. The principal phrases that he claims attest the "homelessness," "lack of family," and "lack of possessions" are repeatedly taken from the same two passages. But the one, that on the calling of the first disciples in Mark 1:16, 20, evidences the lack of home and family only by implication and only temporarily and says nothing about lack of possessions. The other text, Luke 10:4, on the sending of the disciples, says nothing about home or family, although it specifies a temporary lack of certain possessions. The other principal texts Theissen cites in support of the features of his wandering charismatics, such as Mark 10:28–29 or Luke 14:26, are addressed to groups far wider than a handful of itinerants and/or are taken out of context and/or are hyperboles, which Theissen misreads literalistically.

The proof-texts offered for Jesus' and his followers' Cynic lifestyle are no better. Of the two key sayings abstracted from the Q mission discourse, Luke 10:5–6 is not about begging at all, and Luke 10:4, if heard carefully, sounds almost pointedly anti-Cynic. Of the five prohibitions in the reconstructed Q/Luke 10:4, only two, not wearing sandals and not taking money, have Cynic parallels. But Q/Luke 10:4 then prohibits what were perhaps the three most distinguishing characteristics of the Cynic lifestyle: the staff, the bag (*pera*, which was in effect also their begging "bowl"), and, in the prohibition of greeting on the road, the bold speech (*parrēsia*).[6] It should be pointed out, moreover, that there are serious problems of evidence, dating, consistency, and interpretation with regard to our reconstruction of Cynic philosophy itself. What it meant to be a Cynic is not at all clear, particularly for the first century. There is little or no evidence that Cynics were making much of an impact anywhere before late in the first century, and we have no evidence at all for their influence in Galilee. Moreover, Cynicism was primarily an urban phenomenon, while consensus places both the ministry of Jesus and the early Jesus movement in the villages and towns, not cities, of Galilee. For the similarities of certain motifs between Jesus traditions and Cynic discourse and behavior, the obvious explanation is not that Jesus and his followers were Cynics but that "Cynics shared things in common with a broader cross-section of their society."[7]

The fact that the proof-texts offered fail to substantiate the claim that Jesus and his first followers were like Cynic philosophers suggests that the reasons for the attractiveness of the Cynic Jesus lie elsewhere There are some clear reasons why late-twentieth-century Americans, Britishers, and Germans would be intrigued by a Cynic Jesus and his followers. The influence of Bultmann has been pervasive methodologically as well as theologically, and the Cynic Jesus is clearly in the Bultmannian heritage. It is impossible to miss how similar Bultmann's existentialist theology, focused as it was on decision about one's own authentic existence, is to the ancient Cynic philosophy that now fascinates Bultmann's scholarly heirs. The representation of Jesus and his first followers, moreover, was especially attractive in relation to the social-political circumstances in the United States in the 1970s.[8]

Despite the lack of evidence for it in the synoptic Gospels, the hypothesis of the Cynic Jesus is rooted deeply in the established assumptions, concepts, and methods of New Testament studies as a field. The apparent lack of evidence for such a hypothesis suggests that we need to reexamine those assumptions, concepts, and methods. The portrayal of Jesus and his followers as Cynic philosophers may provide a useful case study in how problematic some of our assumptions and methods have become. The obvious place to start is with how Theissen and others read Jesus' sayings.

ASSUMPTIONS AND APPROACHES: A PROBLEMATIC APPROACH TO TEXTS/SAYINGS

Upon close examination of Theissen's presentation of the "wandering charismatics," it is evident that he reads texts in particular ways that might be characterized as follows: (1) literally; (2) addressed to individuals; (3) isolated from literary context, apparently intentionally; (4) without consideration of closely related sayings; (5) without consideration of the past (cultural heritage) and (anticipations about) the future; (6) according to standard concepts in biblical studies that have some rather stark Christian theological biases; (7) without attention to historical social context; (8) without critical awareness of his/our own views and interests. Theissen's way of reading texts, however, is somewhat typical of studies of Jesus and the synoptic Gospel tradition generally. I would like us to review critically these ways of reading Gospel texts. Such a critical review of our approach to texts will lead to possible alternatives that may be more appropriate to those texts and that may yield a very different picture of Jesus. I will review these ways of reading forward, no. 1 through no. 8, then attempt to sketch out an alternative approach "backward," as it were, starting with our own views and working back to the texts.

1. Theissen, along with many others, believes that the sayings of Jesus were meant both seriously and *literally*. "Leave the dead to bury the dead" (Luke 9:59–60) he takes as a command to violate fundamental filial piety addressed to a fellow who wanted to go bury his father who had just died. Following Jesus, he suggests, meant literally to "hate" your father and mother and children and siblings, etc. (Luke 14:26, although apparently the next saying about "bearing your own cross" is not taken so literally!).

2. Reading through the eyes of modern individualists, many interpreters of Jesus' sayings understand them as *addressed to individuals* for implementation in their own individual lifestyle. This makes a considerable difference in how the meaning of particular sayings is construed. For example, reading "do not be anxious about what you shall eat or put on" as addressed to individuals, Theissen, Mack, and others construe the saying as an exhortation to voluntary poverty.

3. Because, in our defensive reaction to enlightenment reasoning, we were suspicious of Gospel narratives as reliable historical evidence for Jesus, and because we thought we could find the original forms of Jesus' sayings, we have intentionally *isolated* particular sayings *from* their *literary context*. But there is simply no such thing as meaning without context. That is especially striking with isolated sayings or aphorisms (no matter how "pithy"), where everything depends on the situation or circumstances of

the people addressed. So what happens when we modern New Testament scholars isolate sayings from literary context? Not having any indication from a text about the context in which particular sayings would have some meaning, we assume or construct a context for the isolated sayings. Theissen *constructs* a context, "itinerant radicalism," for which there is no direct literary evidence, and Downing, Vaage, and Mack, having isolated several sayings from literary context in Matthew, Luke, and Q, then supply the overall picture in which individual sayings are understood from later literature about Cynic philosophers.

One of the standard criteria for establishing the "authentic" sayings of Jesus, the criterion of "dissimilarity," compounds the problem created by isolating the sayings from literary context in the first place. That is, we have been judging sayings as more likely coming from Jesus himself if they are different from traditional Jewish teachings on the one hand and from the products or concerns of the early churches on the other hand. With that procedure we tend to construct a picture of Jesus as an alien to the culture in which he supposedly lived and ministered.

4. In focusing on sayings isolated from literary context, Theissen and others also *leave related sayings* of Jesus *out of account.* For example, they claim that Jesus' call to itinerant radicalism was basically "antifamily" on the basis of the call of the first disciples to leave home and the saying about "hating" mother and father, etc., without taking into consideration the highly positive statements about the family in other sayings, e.g., in Mark 10:2–9, 11–12, 10:29–30, and Luke/Q 16:18. Similarly, they take sayings such as Luke 10:4 and Luke 12:22ff as exhortations to adopt a lifestyle of voluntary poverty without adequate consideration of other sayings (e.g., "blessed are you poor/hungry") in which Jesus appears to be offering the kingdom to people who are concretely hungry and destitute.

5. We often *fail to consider* the historical dimension, *the past* cultural heritage *and/or future* anticipation, that may be implicit or even explicit in sayings. For example, Theissen

reads Mark 10:28–29 without even completing the saying (isolation from literary context!) and without attention to the future anticipation expressed in the full saying, which continues into 10:30: those who leave house and family do so only temporarily, apparently for purpose of mission, in anticipation of the eventual restoration and renewal precisely of house, family, and village life ("now in this age ... with fields and persecutions"). In fact, the very purpose of their temporarily leaving home would appear to be the renewal of family and village life.[9]

6. Synoptic Gospel texts are also often read according to standard concepts of New Testament studies *with Christian theological biases*. Gospel texts, like Pauline letters, it is assumed, are about a transition from one religion or religious self-understanding to another, with no serious political implications involved. Those who now imagine Jesus and his first followers as Cynics either tend to ignore the crucifixion or, like earlier generations of apologetic scholars, explain it as a big mistake. After all, they claim, Jesus was only "mildly subversive," radical only in the sense of being "countercultural" or "unconventional," and did not challenge the basic social structure and religious-political institutions of Jewish Palestine.[10] The prophetic woes against the Pharisees and the prophecies against the Temple, high priests, and Jerusalem are explained as the retaliatory frustrations of Jesus' followers when they came into conflict with the guardians of Jewish conventions (Pharisees). Both Pharisees and Jerusalem are understood as representing "Judaism" or "all Israel." We can readily discern two standard assumptions of our field here: that the principal conflicts in ancient Palestine were (1) that between Judaism and Hellenism, and (2) that between Judaism and the Christian religion emerging from and breaking away from it. And note here that Jesus and his Cynic-like followers stand both on the Hellenism side and on the Christianity side of these divides.[11]

7. We generally read synoptic Gospel texts *without attention to historical social context*, largely because we have

never investigated it very precisely and simply do not know much about it. We still deal in broad general concepts that have little historical basis, such as "Judaism" versus "Hellenism" or "Jewish" versus "Christian." Because we still approach ancient Palestine with such vague general concepts, Cynic-like vagabonds can be imagined in Galilee according to a syllogism of broad generalities: Galilee was "Hellenized," and Cynics were part of Hellenistic culture; therefore there must have been Cynic influence in Galilee.

8. Finally, we regularly read texts *without being critically aware of our own assumptions, views, and interests,* and how these may determine or be served by our interpretations. Insofar as Theissen finds that the most demanding teachings of Jesus pertained only to a handful of "wandering charismatics" in ancient Palestine and not to people involved in ordinary community life, he has relieved the modern Gospel reader involved in ordinary life of taking them very seriously. Or, insofar as Jesus is to be understood as only a "mildly subversive" critic of social conventions, and not a more demanding prophet engaged in serious political conflict, he provides a comfortable prototype for contemporary clergy or professors of theology. In both Bultmann's "demythologizing" project and the new hermeneutic approach designed to overcome the distance between ancient biblical text and today's reader, we have been attempting to translate the Bible into our own terms and culture. But biblical literature and history cannot challenge our assumptions and interests if we do not allow them to stand over against us as literature and history with their own integrity.

TOWARD AN ALTERNATIVE APPROACH

8. In modern America we have certain cherished *assumptions,* among them (a) that religion is a sphere separate from politics and economics; (b) that we live in a classless

society, with a fair degree of equality of opportunity; and (c) that the individual is the primary and important focus of life and meaning. It is just these peculiarly modern Western assumptions that we must question if we are to understand biblical materials and allow them to stand over against us in their own historical context.

7. For the *ancient Palestinian life-world* presupposed and presented in the synoptic Gospels the corresponding realities were very different, almost the converse of our modern assumptions. (a) What we would call religion was inseparable from, indeed embedded with, political-economic forms and structures (e.g., the Temple with its high priesthood was the dominant political-economic as well as religious institution in Jewish Palestine). (b) There was a sharp social (political-economic-religious) division between the rulers (chief priests and scribes based in the Temple as well as the Herodians) and the ruled (the vast majority being peasants in villages and towns). (c) Individuals were basically embedded in the fundamental (corporate) social forms of family and village.[12]

The diversity in late Second Temple Jewish Palestine now being recognized goes far beyond the so-called Jewish sects of Pharisees, Sadducees, and Essenes, who comprised only a tiny fraction of the population near the top of the social pyramid. The diversity in Jewish Palestine had a certain fundamental social structure discernible through literary and archaeological evidence. Two or three salient aspects of this basic social structure are particularly relevant to and understanding of the synoptic Gospel traditions and Jesus. There were differences between village communities, on the one hand, and the capital city in which the ruling institutions and families were situated, on the other. The villagers, moreover, supported the capital city with the tithes and offerings they brought or sent to the Temple and priesthood. Compounding the class differences were the regional differences between Galilee and Jerusalem/Judaea. Galilee had been brought under the control of Jerusalem by the Hasmonean high priestly rulers only about a hundred years before the birth of Jesus. There had been prolonged resistance in Galilee to Herod's conquest of the country in 40–37 B.C.E. and an uprising in the area of Sepphoris and Nazareth when Herod died.

6. Assuming that we should *adjust our conceptual apparatus to the historical realities* of ancient Palestine presupposed and apparently addressed in Jesus' sayings, we can make some conceptual adjustments that correspond to the three realizations just articulated. (a) Since religion did not yet exist as a separable phenomenon, it is inappropriate to speak of "Christianity" or "Judaism," or of the Pharisees or followers of Jesus as if they were a religious "sect" like the early modern Mennonites or Methodists. The sayings and doings of Jesus, like the applications of the Torah espoused by scribes and Pharisees, addressed social relationships generally, not some separable religious aspect of life. (b) The "scribes" and the Pharisees were no more a "middle class" than they were a religious "sect." Rather they were representatives (historical sociologists would say "retainers")[13] of the Temple-based high-priestly government in Jerusalem, charged, among other things, with interpretation of the Torah, which was something like the official "constitution" and "lawbook" through which the Jerusalem government ruled the society. (c) The "synagogues" mentioned in the Gospels were not religious buildings where individuals gathered to worship, on the model of modern churches and synagogues. There is no solid archaeological evidence for synagogue buildings in Galilean towns until well after the time of Jesus. Rather the *synagogai* in the Gospels were the local forms of self-government and community life, assemblies or "town meetings" which conducted everything from regular prayers to repair of the local water supply.

5. Proceeding with this adjusted conceptual apparatus, we can recognize some important aspects of the *people's cultural heritage and anticipations,* again organized corresponding to the above points. (a) The Torah and prophets dealt inseparably with political-economic-

religious matters. (b) Beside or rather underneath the "official tradition," the written Torah and officially sanctioned interpretations cultivated by scribes and Pharisees, there would almost certainly have been what anthropologists have called "little tradition" or popular tradition cultivated among the people. There would almost certainly have been much overlap and a certain interaction between the two levels of tradition, but different emphases and implications. (c) The cultural heritage and anticipations were generally communal, and their application/ implication determined according to the fundamental social forms, primarily family and local (village) community. One of the principal sayings taken by Theissen and others as evidence for the wandering Cynic-like lifestyle turns out rather to illustrate this point about communal anticipations: according to the saying of Jesus in Mark 10:29–30, the very purpose of leaving home and family in order to engage in mission was the renewal of family and village life ("houses, mothers, children, etc., and fields").

4. *Considering sayings of Jesus in relation to one another* ought to be a standard procedural principle. Indeed, once we recognize that meaning is contextual, we would ideally need to consider every saying in relation to all other sayings in order to appreciate where a given saying fits into the overall context of Jesus' ministry. At the very least we must consider sayings that appear to be on the same issue in relation to one another. In regard to the family, for example, once we recognize that Jesus insists upon marriage as the basis of social relations in Mark 10:2–9, 10–12, then related sayings such as Luke 10:4 appear not as antifamily but as instructions for mission, just as the abandonment of homes and families in Mark 10:29 turned out to be for the sake of mission (and only temporary).

3. As noted in the critique above, intentionally isolating the sayings of Jesus from their literary contexts tends toward the determination of the context of meaning by the modern interpreter. But if we want to let Jesus' ministry and the Jesus movement stand over against us, then the

primary means available to us to discern the possible historical social context in which Jesus' sayings and doings resonated are their current *literary contexts in the synoptic Gospels.* Thus, far from isolating sayings from their literary contexts, we must study those contexts and work through them. In this connection we can draw on recent analysis of the Sayings Source Q as a (hypothetical) literary document. That "compositional" analysis of Q indicates that it was not just a collection of independent sayings, but a sequence of discourses, each of which has a particular theme or purpose or function for the communities addressed. Illustrations can best be taken from the literary contexts of sayings central to the case for a Cynic Jesus.

The sayings in Luke 10:4, on what (not) to take on the journey, and in 10:6–7, on eating and lodging, are both embedded in the "mission discourse" in Luke 10:2–16 and, we believe, prior to Luke in the Sayings Source Q. Not only that, but there is a parallel mission discourse in Mark 6:7–13, comparison with which leads us to believe that there must have been an oral prototype of a mission discourse behind both Luke/Q 10:4–11 and Mark 6:8–11. If Q is dated around 50 C.E., then this mission discourse would have been very early indeed, within ten or so years of Jesus' ministry. It stretches the historical imagination beyond credibility, then, to believe that these sayings were originally aphorisms pertaining to an individualistic Cynic-like lifestyle of homeless begging and lack of possessions, and only later were used in the mission discourse. Rather these sayings, from the earliest point we can trace through their current literary contexts in Mark and Q/Luke, must have been integral components of the commissioning of missionaries to heal and preach the Kingdom of God, apparently as an extension of Jesus' own mission.

The sayings about "asking and receiving," etc., in Luke/Q 11:9 taken in isolation are susceptible of being read as a Cynic-like instruction for voluntary poverty and a life of begging. Examination of the same sayings in the Gospel of Thomas 92 and 94 indicates that these brief sayings have virtually no meaning in themselves and are utterly dependent on what they are connected with and how they are understood in a given context. In the Lukan and Q context, however, these sayings are part of an instruction on prayer, on boldly petitioning the Father, the core of which is the Lord's Prayer. Judging from the principal petitions of the Lord's Prayer, however, and going with the reconstruction of the original wording of "forgive us our debts" still present in Matthew, the people here instructed to pray are apparently hungry and indebted, i.e., already dirt poor and just longing for a better future, and not the sort of people who needed an exhortation to voluntary poverty. Given that the significance of these sayings is so dependent on the context in which they are used, we should yield to the context indicated in Luke, Matthew, and Q — that is, exhortation of poor people to petition God boldly for the necessities of life — rather than a recent scholarly construct.

2. These same passages also illustrate that there are no indications in the actual texts that Jesus' sayings were addressed to individuals about their own individual lifestyle. These particular sayings and most others were rather addressed to a wider group of people, most of them apparently people of modest circumstances. Reading sayings as addressed to *individuals* for implementation in their own individual lifestyles simply forgets or abandons the insights of form-criticism, that *the use and transmission of sayings had a social or community context.* Even the most clearly "sapiential" teachings are community-directed, some of them obviously pertaining to social interaction: e.g., "turn the other cheek," etc., in Luke 6:27–36; or "do not be anxious about what you shall put on ... " in 12:22. The implication of how we read makes a big difference in what the saying is understood to mean. Addressed to an individual, the saying "do not be anxious about what you shall put on, etc." could be an exhortation to voluntary poverty. Addressed to a group of people it pertained to their concrete situation of poverty and hunger. Many of Jesus' sayings

pertain to social relations, sometimes local economic relations such as borrowing and lending, other times relations
between the people and the rulers or their "retainers."
Thus we must attend to the social relations indicated in the
sayings, and that in the broader literary context and in the
historical social context.

1. Language is a social phenomenon. Greater attention to the literary and historical social contexts will also
help us discern just how language is being used in social relations with subtleties and overtones. Now it is very
difficult to imagine that either Jesus or his followers understood sayings such as "leave the dead to bury the dead"
or "hate your father and mother" literally. (Is an enthusi-
astic football fan who shouts "get out there and kill 'em"
really exhorting the team on the field to commit murder?)
Language is a highly flexible and versatile means of com-
municating in any number of ways that are not literal.
Many of Jesus' sayings were clearly nonliteral uses of language
such as metaphor (e.g., "you are the salt of the earth"), hyperbole (e.g., "leave the dead to bury the dead," "hate your
father and mother," etc.), or curses ("Woe to you . . . ").

THE RENEWAL, NOT THE JUDGMENT, OF ISRAEL

These criteria or steps can be used as an alternative approach to several sets of Jesus sayings. Focusing on the
same material used for the Cynic portrayal of Jesus, i.e.,
the Synoptic Sayings Source Q, should illuminate how the
same material can appear very different when approached
with alternative assumptions and procedures. In keeping
with point 3 above we must deal not with isolated sayings but with whole sets of sayings or discourses, which
comprise the immediate literary context of particular sayings.[14] For example, instead of taking Luke/Q 10:4 out of
literary context, we will consider the "mission discourse"
in Luke/Q 10:2–16 as a whole, including what appears to

be the introductory sayings for that discourse in Luke/Q 9:57–62. Or, instead of taking Luke 12:22 out of literary context, we will consider the whole discourse on anxiety in Luke/Q 12:22–31. Then in keeping with point 4 above we must make regular comparisons with material in Mark and other Gospel sources, since good historical method requires comparison of our principal sources and their representations of Jesus.[15] The result will be a sketch of Jesus that makes him appear as a prophet engaged in the renewal of the people of Israel.

In the mission discourse, both in Q (Luke/Q 10:2–16) and in Mark (6:7–13), Jesus charges his disciples to continue his own ministry of healing/exorcising and preaching the kingdom. Nothing in either version of the mission discourse indicates that the mission is to gentiles. The mission is apparently directed to the people of Israel. From the instruction for curses against unreceptive towns or places in both versions of the discourse (Luke/Q 10:10–11; Mark 6:11) we can tell that the envoys are sent not simply to particular households, where they are to stay and take meals, but to whole villages or towns. The series of sayings placed just prior to the mission instructions in Q, if we do not read them literally and as isolated sayings directed to individual potential "followers," may help us understand the character of the mission and of Jesus' ministry. The sayings in Luke 9:57–62 are reminiscences of or allusions to Elijah's call of Elisha. That suggests rather unmistakably that the mission is analogous to the prophetic mission of the renewal of Israel for which Elijah commissioned Elisha. It is worth noting that Mark not only represents the miracles of Jesus as an Elijah-like and Moses-like ministry of renewal of the people through healings and feedings and sea-crossings,[16] but also, in the "transfiguration" story, dramatically associates Jesus with Elijah and Moses, the great prophetic prototypes who founded and renewed the people, according to Israelite tradition.

That the ministry of Jesus was understood as the renewal of the people of Israel is indicated repeatedly in both Q and Mark and Jesus is represented in prophetic terms throughout much of the synoptic Gospel tradition. Throughout Q there are many references to Israelite tradition, whether to the ancestors Abraham, Isaac, and Jacob or to events and figures cited as historical examples, such as Sodom, Jonah and the Ninevites, and Solomon and the queen of the South. But far from being learned scribal quotations from the official Torah, these are simply allusions probably stemming from popular tradition.

Perhaps the most important Q passage in this connection is the often misunderstood and mistranslated saying that apparently formed the closing section of the Sayings Source:

Truly I tell you, at the renewal of all things, when the Son of Man is seated on the throne of his glory, you who have followed me will also sit on twelve thrones, judging the twelve tribes of Israel. (Matt. 19:28)	You are those who have stood by me in my trials; and I confer on you, just as my Father has conferred on me, a kingdom, so that you may eat and drink at my table in my kingdom, and you will sit on thrones judging the twelve tribes of Israel. (Luke 22:28–30)

This passage is a "textbook" case of how exegesis is often determined by Christian theological schemes, and in this case even the latest translation, the NRSV, perpetuates a now traditional mistranslation. The christological image of Jesus as the future "Son of Man" coming for "the last judgment" at the "end of the world" (rooted particularly in Matthew 25) has heavily influenced what may have been the Q version of the saying.[17]

The key mistranslation that has skewed the reading of the saying, however, is that of *krinein* as "judging." Ironically, the *Theological Dictionary of the New Testament,* which is often overly determined by Christian theological conceptions, presents an unusually critical review of the actual biblical use of language in this case. Despite their ordinary juridical sense of "judging," or "deciding," *krinein,* etc., and the Hebrew terms behind them, *sapat*, etc., go beyond the standard Greek meaning of *krinein* and must be differentiated from the idea of distributive justice or the Roman concept of law. In fact, these terms in biblical usage, depending upon the context, carry the sense of defense, deliverance, even of "establishing justice for." We need only call to mind many familiar passages in the Psalms to recognize the problem of meaning in Luke 22:28–30: how misleading it would be to translate passages such as Psalms 10:18, 72:4, 76:9, 82:3, 103:6, 140:12, or 146:7 as if God were "judging" the poor, the hungry, or the oppressed of the earth, or "judging" the orphan and widow. Further, the servant of Yahweh, who is to restore the twelve tribes of Israel in Isaiah 49:6, is expected to bring "justice," not "judgment" to the peoples in Isaiah 42:1.

The positive and active sense of *sapat* and *krinein* as "establishing justice for" or "delivering" in the Psalms and Servant Songs should help us read Luke 22:28–30 more appropriately. This last section in Q is not about the Twelve "judging" Israel. It is rather a final promising declaration that the Twelve will be delivering or effecting justice for the twelve tribes of Israel. Moreover, if instead of applying the criterion of dissimilarity, we looked for ways in which such a declaration would fit into the historical situation of the people in ancient Palestine under Roman rule, two passages indicate that other groups had parallel expectations. In the Psalms of Solomon 17:28–32, the anointed son of David will "effect justice for" or "deliver" the tribes of the people. And in the Community Rule from the Dead Sea Scrolls found at Qumran (1QS 8:1–4), the representative "twelve men and three priests" who comprise the "Council of the Community" are to effect "righteousness, justice, lovingkindness, and humility,...preserve the faith in the land,...and atone for sin by the practice of justice."

That Jesus and the twelve are to restore or renew Israel and not "judge" can become ever clearer by rereading some other Q sayings that have often been misunderstood. The prophetic lament that Jesus delivers against Jerusalem,

Luke/Q 13:34–35, has been read particularly by German Christian scholars as a judgment against "Judaism" or "all Israel." But that reading imposes on Q and the early Jesus movement a later Christian theological scheme of history whereby God was understood to have judged Jews and Judaism because of their failure to accept Jesus as the Messiah. But "messiah" as a title or theme is not even present in Q, and there is no reason whatever to take "Jerusalem" as a symbol for "all Israel" in Luke 13:34–35. As we have noted above, at the time Q was supposedly composed in Palestine, the principal social-cultural division was between the rulers, largely in Jerusalem, and the ruled, including those in Galilee. The division ran between Jewish rulers in Jerusalem and Israelites under their rule, while the split between "Jews" and "Christians" had not yet developed. Thus the saying in Luke/Q 13:34–35 is a prophetic lament by a Galilean prophet against the Jewish ruling house in Jerusalem. As with the declaration that the Twelve would be effecting justice for Israel, so in the case of Jesus' prophetic lament over Jerusalem we have a parallel from contemporary Palestinian society. Josephus gives a lengthy report about another rustic prophet named Jesus, son of Hananiah, who repeatedly delivered a lament about the imminent destruction of Jerusalem (*Jewish War* 6.300–309).

This helps clarify another saying apparently in the same Q discourse, a passage usually read according to the Matthean version that makes it apparently a division between Jews and gentile Christians. But if Luke/Q 13:28–29 is read as part of a discourse against the rulers in Jerusalem as well as in the historical context of ancient Palestine, with its principal division being between rulers and ruled, then like the many prophetic passages to which it alludes, it is a declaration that when Israelites gather "from east and west and from north and south" for the banquet of the kingdom with Abraham, Isaac, and Jacob (and the prophets), the rulers will find themselves thrust out. The parable of the great supper, which apparently formed part of the same discourse in Q, Luke 14:16–24, can be read in the same way as a prophetic statement against the wealthy and powerful Jerusalem elite who presume their own privilege. Jesus' mission of renewal for the people of Israel involved prophetic judgment against the rulers in Jerusalem. Again there are exact parallels in Mark, including the thrice-mentioned prophecy of the destruction of the Temple and the prophetic parable of the wicked tenants (= the high priests) who mismanage the Lord's vineyard (= Israel) in 12:1–9.

Yet another discourse in Q that is misunderstood when read according to modern presuppositions and a Christian theological scheme is the set of woes against the Pharisees in Luke/Q 11:39–52. These woes are mistaken as a condemnation of Judaism generally mainly because we identified the Pharisees as representative or typical of Judaism, without taking into account that what we usually think of as "Judaism," a distinctive religious system articulated by the rabbis, did not emerge until several centuries later. On the assumption that we are dealing with religion as a separate dimension of life and that the Pharisees were principally concerned with rituals, these woes are read as a criticism of the Pharisees obsession with legalism, particularly the purity codes. But only two of the woes, 11:39 (cleansing the cup) and 11:44 (unmarked graves) even mention purity concerns, and those only as rhetorical castigation, and the only woe that could possibly refer to the Law is about tithes, which are taxes (i.e., a political-economic as well as religious issue), not purity rituals. If we read the woes more carefully it becomes clear that Jesus is delivering a series of prophetic indictments against the scribes and Pharisees for the deleterious effect they have on the people in pursuing their social role as representatives and interpreters of the Temple government and the official Torah.

A critical rereading of Mark 7:1–23, another passage often misread as concerned primarily with cleanliness codes, and Mark 12:38–13:2 will reveal the same concern: the

primary thrust of the passage is Jesus' condemnation of
the scribes and Pharisees for the disastrous effect that they
have on poor people as representatives of the Temple government (encouraging people to give to the Temple, which
means they do not have enough left to support themselves and their families). That is, again Jesus' concern
for the renewal of the people of Israel entails prophetic
pronouncements against the scribes and Pharisees as representatives of the Jerusalem-based system that "loads
people with burdens hard to bear," exacerbating their situation of poverty and hunger.

JESUS' PROPHETIC RENEWAL OF ISRAEL
IN NEW COVENANTAL COMMUNITY

Other key passages used to construct a Cynic-like picture
of Jesus turn out to represent rather a prophetic ministry
to local community renewal when read according to our
alternative approach. As touched on briefly above, when
read in literary context, less individualistically, and more
concretely, Luke/Q 11:9–13 and 12:22–31 cannot be admo-
nitions to voluntary poverty. Once Luke/Q 12:22–31 is no
longer read in its Lucan resetting as concerned with "possessions" (see Luke 12:32–33), it clearly addresses ordinary
people's anxieties about the basic necessities of life such as
food and clothing. Their links with the Lord's Prayer and
with the rhetorical questions about good gifts of food indicate that the sayings about seeking and finding, etc., in
Luke/Q 11:9–13 were addressed to people who were concretely poor and hungry. The prayer for the kingdom in
Luke/Q 11:2–4 that links the people's own forgiveness of
debts with God's forgiveness of debts clearly indicates a
local community situation including people who are indebted to one another, probably economically as well as
figuratively.

   I have argued before that the set of sayings about
"love your enemies," etc., is addressed to just such lo-

cal community situation.[18] Indeed, the whole "inaugural sermon" in Q, Luke/Q 6:20–29, appears to be addressed to communities of people defined by circumstances of poverty, hunger, and sorrow, as indicated in the opening beatitudes. In more precise terms, the sayings in Luke 6:27–38, 41–42 address such people who, because of their burdensome circumstances of mutual indebtedness and acute anxiety, are faced with unmanageable tensions and the disintegration of social relations in their local communities. But there is even more in this "inaugural sermon" if we have "eyes to see."

If we break with the habit of reading this material as wisdom teachings to abstract individuals in general or, with Theissen and others, to "wandering charismatics" or Cynic-like vagabonds in particular, and recognize just how concrete some of the references in these sayings are, we may also be able to discern what the allusions of particular sayings and the pattern in the whole discourse suggest: this is renewed Israelite covenantal teaching. In several of the sayings in 6:27–36 there are clear allusions to traditional covenantal instructions such as those reflected in the official tradition, the Torah, as well, particularly Leviticus 19. Included are instructions on certain local social-economic problems, such as what to do about one's enemy's ass or ox in distress (see Exod. 23:4–5; Deut. 22:1–4; Sir. 29:1). In closely related later "Christian" literature such as Didache 1–2 and Matthew 5 these same sayings are clustered with stipulations from the Decalogue itself and other traditional covenantal instructions. Moreover, we could make extensive comparisons with explicitly covenantal documents such as the Community Rule from the Dead Sea Scrolls of the Qumran community.

If this "inaugural sermon" is indeed renewed covenantal instruction addressed to local community life, we can take an important step further in discerning what the Sayings Source Q is all about. Insofar as local village communities were the fundamental social form in which the people of Israel were constituted (it was not anything

like what we presuppose in our pluralistic society!), such
covenantal instruction is precisely how one would proceed
on an overall program for the renewal of Israel. Just as
the presence of "the Kingdom of God," which forms the
recurrent and dominant theme in Q, apparently means, socially, the renewal of Israel in Q, so the renewal of Israel
means the renewal of Israelite covenantal justice in local
communities. "The Sermon on the Mount" in Matthew
5–7 only makes schematically explicit what was already
evident in Q.

Lest we think that this renewed or new covenant is
peculiar to Q, we should note the same theme that is recurrent in Mark. The story of the last supper in Mark 14:22–25
juxtaposes a renewal of the covenant with the advent of the
Kingdom of God. In Mark 7:1–23, moreover, Jesus is not de-
bating with the Pharisees about the Torah, but is insisting
on basic covenantal "commands of God" as what should
govern local familial and community relations, in opposition to the Pharisees' traditions, which apparently enjoyed
official status or sanction.

JESUS AS SOCIAL PROPHET

The upshot of this brief survey is that, approached in less
problematic and more appropriate ways, the very sayings
used to construct a Cynic Jesus suggest rather a Jesus
who stands in the tradition of Israelite prophets. Read
in the literary (and social) context of Q discourses, with
comparisons from Mark, these sayings represent Jesus as
engaged in a mission of proclaiming (and demonstrating
through healings) the Kingdom of God to Israel, giving
covenantal teachings to restore just social relations to local
communities in which the people were embedded, offering
assurances and encouragement to a despairing people, and
pronouncing woes and judgment against the rulers and
their representatives. Yet Jesus clearly transcends the role
of an ordinary prophet precisely because he has brought

the Kingdom of God, which means the restoration of the people of Israel. As John the Baptist declares at the beginning of Q, Jesus is the "stronger one" coming who would bring both renewal (through the Holy Spirit) and judgment (with fire). He has the special role of mediator with God (Luke/Q 10:21–24) and receives the sovereignty and passes it on to the people now being renewed (Luke/Q 22:28–30).

The fullest representation of Jesus' role and significance comes in Luke/Q 7:18–35. Jesus affirms that he is indeed the one who is to come, in whose healings and preaching the prophecies and longings of personal and social renewal (allusions to Isaiah) are being fulfilled (7:18–23). Yet that Jesus, while obviously a prophet bringing fulfillment, far transcends the role of any ordinary prophet is indicated in the next set of sayings focused on John's significance (7:24–28). John was a prophet — more than a prophet, in fact, even the messenger (Elijah) prophesied by Malachi. But even this greatest figure in history so far does not compare to the least in the Kingdom of God. Implicit, of course, is that if John was more than a prophet, how much more extraordinary is Jesus, who preaches and manifests the kingdom. Yet Jesus, while transcendent, is still clearly a prophetic figure parallel to John in this discourse, an impression confirmed in the next set of sayings, which concludes with the declaration that "wisdom is vindicated by all her works/children" (7:31–35).

Q thus apparently understands Jesus as the climactic figure in the long line of Israelite prophets. This is implied in Jesus' lament over Jerusalem, Luke/Q 13:34–35 and particularly in the wisdom oracle in Luke/Q 11:49–51. The latter also implies that the death of Jesus was understood as that of a prophetic martyr. The theme of the historical killing of the prophets occurs in both passages as well as in Luke 11:47–48. But the key saying is wisdom's oracle: "I will send them prophets... some of whom they will kill... that the blood of all the prophets... may be required of this generation... " (11:49–51). In context this saying suggests that the prophets sent and killed are John and

Jesus and that the guilt that merits the condemnation of "this generation," apparently the scribes and Pharisees, is their complicity in the killing of Jesus, who must be the climactic and decisive prophet. Thus, although there is no explicit statement about Jesus' death elsewhere in Q (but cf. Luke/Q 14:27), Luke 11:49–51 appears to represent Jesus as the climactic figure in the series of martyred prophets.

If I can venture a bold hypothesis without having space to explore it further, the only major components of the synoptic Gospel (and closely related) traditions that cannot be readily explained as rooted in a *prophetic* ministry or an obvious outgrowth of it are the crucifixion-resurrection kerygma, the passion narrative in Mark, and both the royal (Messiah) and "Son of Man" christologies (Mark, Matthew) — ironically the very components that have been most prominent in subsequent Christian ritual, theology, and general New Testament studies. Yet it seems clear that any of those major components not rooted in the prophetic role can easily be understood as an interpretation of the significance of Jesus' death, or rather, death and vindication, independent of his ministry. Mark's genius was to weave the nonprophetic components together with the traditions of Jesus' prophetic ministry, while the Synoptic Sayings Source provides a set of discourses enabling us to imagine how the Jesus prophetic saying and covenantal teachings could have been components of a prophetic mission of social renewal in Galilee. But I see no evidence that Cynics or wandering charismatics were anywhere in sight.

NOTES

1. Gerd Theissen, *Sociology of Early Palestinian Christianity* (Philadelphia: Fortress, 1978), 8.
2. Ibid., 15.
3. Gerd Theissen, "Itinerant Radicalism: The Tradition of Jesus Sayings from the Perspective of the Sociology of Literature," in *The Bible and Liberation: A Radical Religion Reader*

(Berkeley, Calif.: Community for Religious Research and Education, 1976), 87.

4. The following sketch is heavily indebted to the work of Abraham J. Malherbe, *The Cynic Epistles: A Study Edition* (Missoula, Mont.: Scholars Press, 1977); and "Self-Definition among Epicureans and Cynics," in *Jewish and Christian Self-Definition*, vol. 3, ed. Ben F. Meyer and E. P. Sanders (Philadelphia: Fortress, 1982), 46–59.

5. Characterizations of Jesus and/or his early followers as Cynics are principally by F. Gerald Downing, in a series of articles, as well as in *Jesus and the Threat of Freedom* (London, 1987); *Christ and the Cynics: Jesus and Other Radical Preachers in First-Century Tradition*, JSOT Manuals 4 (Sheffield: JSOT Press, 1988); Burton L. Mack, *A Myth of Innocence: Mark and Christian Origins* (Philadelphia: Fortress, 1988), especially 67–69; Leif Vaage, "The Ethics of an Itinerant Intelligence," Ph.D. diss., Claremont Graduate School, 1987.

6. See further my critique in *Sociology and the Jesus Movement* (New York: Crossroad, 1989), 116–19.

7. See further the judicious, documented criticism of several key facets of the "Cynic" hypothesis by C. M. Tuckett, "A Cynic Q," *Biblica* 70 (1989): 349–76, quotation from 354.

8. Theissen's original article on "Itinerant Radicalism" was published in 1973 (in German, with the English translation in 1975, with the book following in 1978). It may have seemed to provide a certain scriptural legitimation for religiously motivated civil rights and anti–Vietnam War activists who had sacrificed home, family, and remunerative careers for more compelling commitments. On closer examination, of course, it is evident that those who supposedly heeded Jesus' call to an "itinerant radicalism" were not engaged in anything analogous to peace demonstrations or civil rights work. The lifestyle of the "wandering charismatics" (as sketched by Theissen and others) was apparently an end in itself, more analogous to that of the "hippies." Also, it is not surprising that a Cynic Jesus would be attractive to certain university scholars who cultivate a more sophisticated countercultural lifestyle.

9. An illustration for the importance of past heritage can also illustrate the importance of literary context for understanding Jesus' sayings. Luke 9:57–58, 59–60, taken in isolation from literary context and cultural heritage, are read by Theissen and others as sayings about individual discipleship and even as the sharp repartee of a Cynic. But note the literary context in Luke: the preface to the mission discourse! That was apparently the

literary context in Q as well. The sayings were apparently linked
with mission instead of or more than discipleship. The saying in
9:61–62 is only in Luke, so not clearly in Q. But whether or not
it was in Q, its clear allusion to Elijah's call of Elisha to prophetic mission leads us to see that the "leave the dead to
bury the dead" is also an allusion to Elijah's call of Elisha to
prophetic mission. Far more than individual discipleship is involved in this saying if only we do not isolate it and prevent
ourselves from discerning the all-important rich associations
and connections.

10. Mack, *A Myth of Innocence*, 64–69.

11. Few people would have thought that Ronald Reagan
was condemning "all America" when he condemned "Wash-
ington" and government bureaucrats. Correspondingly, there
appears little or no reason to assume that Jesus' sayings against
Jerusalem or woes against the scribes and Pharisees who worked
as interpreters of the constitution and lawbook of the Jewish
Temple-state were condemnations of "Judaism" generally or "all
Israel." New Testament studies are still struggling with the anti-
Judaism it has inherited not simply from German scholarship
but from church "fathers" such as Eusebius.

12. I have taken a few faltering steps toward a new sketch
of the fundamental historical social structure in Palestine in
Sociology and the Jesus Movement, chaps. 4 and 5.

13. See Anthony J. Saldarini, *Pharisees, Scribes, and Sadducees
in Palestinian Society: A Sociological Approach* (Wilmington, Del.:
Michael Glazier, 1988).

14. While careful critical reconstruction of the hypothetical
text of "Q" is being worked out by the International Q Project,
provisional reconstructions are available. See especially John S.
Kloppenborg, *Q Parallels: Synopsis, Critical Notes, and Concordance*
(Sonoma, Calif.: Polebridge, 1988). Even Kloppenborg's critical
synopsis, however, still does not present "Q" in complete discourses, but in sections of discourses, perhaps because of the
logistics of printing. I have argued that Q is not a collection of
sayings but a series of discourses in "*Logoi Propheton?* Reflections
on the Genre of Q," in *The Future of Early Christianity: Essays in
Honor of Helmut Koester,* ed. B. A. Pearson et al. (Minneapolis:
Fortress, 1991), 195–209.

15. I have attempted to combine these two key procedu-
ral principles in analysis of Q in "Q and Jesus: Assumptions,
Approaches, and Analyses," *Semeia* 55 (*Early Christianity, Q, and
Jesus*), 175–209.

16. Research on the miracle chains in and behind Mark is

summarized and consolidated by Mack, *A Myth of Innocence,* chap. 8.

17. I made a more detailed treatment of this passage in *Jesus and the Spiral of Violence: Popular Jewish Resistance in Roman Palestine* (San Francisco: Harper & Row, 1987; Minneapolis: Fortress, 1992), 199–208.

18. See "Ethics and Exegesis: 'Love Your Enemies' and the Doctrine of Non-Violence," *JAAR* 54 (1986): 3–31; and *Jesus and the Spiral of Violence,* 259–73.

Chapter 4

Jesus and the Politics of His Day

Doron Mendels

The political Jesus was, and still, is a burning topic in scholarship of the New Testament.[1] Strangely enough, historians who deal with the history of the Second Temple period do not give enough attention to the problem of the politics of early Christianity.[2] One of the reasons is that historians usually dismiss the narrative parts of the New Testament as "religious documents" that have no significant value for the "real" historian.[3] This is true not only of Jewish scholars, but also of some of my Christian friends who cannot understand how a "serious" historian (like me...) believes in the historicity of certain parts of the New Testament. But what do we mean by "historicity"? For myself as a historian the three synoptic Gospels, John, and Acts, reflect the expressed awareness of their own history of various groups in the first century C.E.. As a historian of antiquity (not only of Jewish and Early Christian history) I can say that many of the traditions found in the narrative parts of the New Testament go back to the 30s and 40s of the first century C.E., while some reflect an awareness of what these years meant in the communities some years later. But the great historian Josephus also reflects in his writings a similar consciousness *post eventum*.[4] The narrative parts of the New Testament, as I have shown elsewhere, are much closer to the "history" found in Josephus's *Antiquities* 1–11 than to "creative" historiography that was fashionable in the ancient Near East at the time. Both Josephus and Luke make a statement that they are going to relate the "truth." In short, the narrative in the New Testament reflects the *Zeitgeist* of the first century C.E. in the same manner as Josephus does.[5]

I am of course aware of the different tendentious approaches to be found in the synoptic Gospels and in John. Yet they all, I believe, reflect a Palestinian *Sitz im Leben* that was in certain instances transmitted and filtered through the Diaspora communities or through the communities that were situated in Greek cities of Palestine.[6] Hence, when I mention the political Jesus, I wish to see him conceptually and ideologically within the Judaism of the Palestine of his day, although I would not exclude altogether Diaspora Judaism as a background to Jesus' community. It is known that many Jews in the Greek cities of Palestine lived their daily lives in a Diaspora situation.

POLITICS AND THE KINGDOM OF GOD

What then is meant by "political"? Borg and Horsley tackled this problem again in the 1980s in a very interesting manner.[7] I should like to clarify the picture by adding that it would be entirely wrong to speak of a clear-cut dichotomy between political and religious within the context of the Hellenistic Near East. It would perhaps be more appropriate to make a dividing line between *earthly* and *spiritual*. We can thus speak of "earthly politics" and "spiritual politics," because the world of Judaism from which Jesus' community emerged was dualistic: there were both earthly and heavenly politics, if one can express it thus. Take for instance the Psalter, where in many psalms God is described in terms similar to those used later for the "On

Kingship" documents, which were very much "earthly political" (Psalm 47, for instance).

But let me be more concrete and discuss the problem of kingship in Jesus' world, because kingship is a cornerstone in the politics of that time. As a historian I am not interested in theological speculations, but rather I am interested in what the texts reveal when examined in the context of the historical background. In other words, when Jesus uses the term "Kingdom of God," he uses a political term "kingdom" (*malkuta* in Aramaic, *basileia* in Greek). Was Jesus then "earthly political" or "spiritually political"? Or perhaps the transmitters of the traditions (Mark, Matthew, etc.) invented the *basileia tou theou* ("Kingdom of God") and gave it an *interpretatio Graeca,* as some scholars would like to believe? Hence two worlds should be considered: the world of Judaism and the world of Hellenism, which surrounded Judaism at that time. Let us start with the second.

According to most traditions, when Jesus refers to the Kingdom of God he uses terms that are taken from the current vocabulary of earthly kingship that we can find in documents and inscriptions of the Hellenistic Near East, for instance, *euergetes, pater.* However, Greek notions of kingship, which in many ways influenced the Near East, are often associated with clear-cut programs concerning a new future order. (The Greeks did not believe in eschatology because their concept of politics was circular, while that of Judaism and Christianity was linear.) Plato's *Republic* and the programs of the early stoa and Hellenistic utopists can be brought as examples. The Greeks were perhaps less dualistic than the Jews in their concepts of kingship, but in the Hellenistic period they still viewed their gods as being like kings (Euhemerism).[8] No saying of Jesus contains anything of that sort. In his parables, it is true, there are suggestions about the candidates eligible for the Kingdom, but he never gives a clear picture of the Kingdom of God in line with Greek or Hellenistic programs. Thus the concept of the *basileia tou theou* and the *basileia tōn ouranōn* does not derive from the pagan world, even if the evangelists, or whoever transmitted the traditions, were influenced by Greek culture.

With what does it in fact have contact? The Jewish concepts of the "Kingdom of God" go back, as everyone knows, to the Hebrew Bible (*malkuth shamayim*). The Jews of the period under discussion have a very clear dualistic world consisting of the Kingdom of God in heaven (which might become earthly in the *eschaton*, the end of days), and the earthly kingship. It is quite clear that Jesus, as he is portrayed in the Gospels, had this kind of kingdom in mind, with the additions and embellishments of the intertestamental period. According to all the traditions Jesus was against earthly kingship of any sort and reverted to heavenly kingship. The reason for this was that all forms of rulership were anathema for most religious Jews in the Judaism of the time from Herod to his successors. Let us go into more detail regarding the Jewish background.

BACKGROUND TO THE IDEA OF KINGDOM OF GOD

First, a Kingdom of God was depicted in a very interesting document that was published recently. *The Songs of the Sabbath Sacrifice*, which was composed at some time in the second or first century B.C.E., anticipates Jesus' Kingdom of God.[9] It states that God is the king who sits on a throne of honor in a Heavenly Temple and has a heavenly army at his disposal. This is in line with the famous Psalm 47, mentioned above, where God is depicted as an earthly king, who maintains a universal rule over all the nations.

Second, from the Jewish Diaspora we have another piece of information that is no less interesting for our case. This is the famous depiction of Moses' kingship by Ezekiel the Tragedian, which reads as follows (third century B.C.E.):

I dreamt there was on the summit of mount Sinai
A certain great throne extending up to heaven's cleft,

On which there sat a certain noble man
Wearing a crown and holding a great sceptre
In his left hand. With his right hand
He beckoned to me, and I stood before the throne.
He gave me the sceptre and told me to sit
On the great throne. He gave me the royal crown
And he himself left the throne.

I beheld the entire circled earth
Both beneath the earth and above the heaven,
And a host of stars fell on its knees before me;
I numbered them all,
They passed before me like a squadron of soldiers.
Then, seized with fear, I rose from my sleep.

His father-in-law interprets the dream thus:
O friend, that which God has signified to you as good;
Might I live until the time when these things happen to you.
Then you will raise up a great throne
And it is you who will judge and lead humankind;
As you beheld the whole inhabited earth,
the things beneath and the things above God's heaven,
So will you see things present, past, and future.

In this scene Moses receives his kingship from God, and there is no doubt that he becomes a kind of universal king.[10] There are scholars who wish to see in it a replica of Alexander's visit to the Temple of Amon, where he received the world kingship from the god Amon. One can also look at Moses' kingship against the political background of Ptolemaic Egypt.

Ptolemaic kingship had a very strong universalistic flavor. Ptolemy was equated with Dionysus and with Osiris, the deceased king, both of whom were universal king-gods. The Jews living under Ptolemaic kings (either in Egypt or in its possessions outside Egypt, namely, Palestine, Cyrene, Cyprus, and other places) could not identify themselves with kings who were seen as gods (as, for instance, we know from the Book of 3 Maccabees). The indigenous population in Egypt viewed their Greek kings as pharaohs, that is, as Egyptian gods such as Amon and Horus; and their deceased kings were seen to be like Osiris.

The Greeks in Egypt viewed the Ptolemies as Greek gods, e.g., Dionysus, Heracles, Zeus, and others. What could pious Jews (and Ezekiel was a pious Jew) who were Egyptians do in this situation? They could not identify with the pagan gods, yet they had to identify with some king associated with Egypt because they wanted to be considered as part of the Egyptian "nation." They therefore turned to their past and within this framework "invented" their own king, an Egyptian Hebrew, who received his kingship from the king of kings, God, just as the Ptolemies had received their kingship from their own gods. A precedent was thereby created in which pious Jews showed their own "national" god as being a universalistic God (whose dominion therefore also included Egypt).

This is perhaps the closest we come to the association between a king and a past political and spiritual leader of the nation of Israel. This also brings us to the question of the king-Messiah, the son of another famous political figure, David. Needless to say, the figure of David, the king of Israel, was imbued with strong political overtones at the time under discussion. Hence, was the "earthly political" in its historical dimension (figure of David), important as a source of inspiration for Jesus and for his historians? Let us discuss this further.[11]

THE KING-MESSIAH IN ISRAEL

The figure of the Messiah that emerges from the literature that came subsequent to the Roman conquest of Palestine (63 B.C.E.), takes two different forms.[12] First there is the political figure of Messiah, the son of David, and second the transcendental Messiah, who is dissociated from any real physical kingship. Let us start with the first, probably the more popular form, the one of the Messiah, the son of David. It is found in Jewish sources of the time (Psalms of Solomon 17) and even more frequently mentioned in the Gospels. There the son of David seems to appear as the most attractive alternative to earthly Hellenistic kings in general and the reality of the decaying kingship of the Herodian dynasty in particular. Thus, even if these texts were put in writing after 70 C.E., the vicissitudes of the Herodian dynasty formed their background. The association with the son of David took people's minds back to King David and his son Solomon and their achievements in the past history of Israel.

It is therefore important to examine briefly how the literature of the time coped with the figures of these two kings. A great deal can be learned about what people at the time thought of kingship from the various interpretations of David and Solomon. Two questions present themselves: (a) Why was the messiah figure associated with David? and (b) since the messiah figure was associated with the present and the future both in Christianity and Judaism, why do both religions look back to the past in their desire to welcome the *eschaton* (end of the days)?

David and Solomon were the most important national figures in Israel's past. They were Jewish kings in their own right and held Jewish sovereignty over the whole land, subjugating all the foreigners in it and even some outside of it. David conquered Jerusalem, defeating the Jebusites, and Solomon built the Temple. During their reigns the Israelite kingdom was united; it was in fact the only time in Jewish history when "Israelites" were referred to and when the term denotes in fact the whole nation settled on the land. At that time there was no meaningful Israelite diaspora outside Palestine. David founded the first legitimate Israelite dynasty, and, in retrospect, this was the ideal kingship the Jews had always wanted. Additionally, David was depicted by the Scriptures as a poet and a musician, and Solomon was shown as a wise man to whom the whole world looked for advice. Josephus, in his *Antiquities*, expressed his generation's appreciation of these traits. The Jews and early Christians of the first century C.E. — people who knew and remembered their past daily — could not help thinking in a nostalgic manner about David and Solomon.[13] What they had in their daily life they believed was merely a mockery of a real king.

It seems then that many Jewish groups at the time wanted to return to Jewish kingship as it had been in the days of David and Solomon, and Jewish liturgy of later periods shows this desire very clearly. Thus it is no wonder that some of Jesus' followers identified him with a political figure who would restore the political grandeur of Israel's past. They called him "ben David." Some of the later redactors also interpreted his role as being "ben David" when they composed the famous genealogies going back to David. However, the fact that David and Solomon were in the main associated with politics brought about opposition to them and the adherence to the more transcendental king and the Messiah who was spiritual and not connected with the Davidic house.

Thus the second aspect of messianism was a transcendental one. The belief that Jesus was a messiah who was spiritual can be traced back to the Gospels themselves, in which we find many of the current Palestinian traditions. For instance, Matthew 20:20–28 shows that there was opposition to a real king. Jesus said to his disciples (vv. 25–28):

> You know that the rulers of the gentiles [*hoi archontes ton ethnon*] lord it over them, and their great men [*hoi megaloi*] exercise authority over them. It shall not be so among you; but whoever would be great among you must be your servant, and whoever would be first among you must be your slave; even as the Son of Man came not to be served but to serve, and to give his life as ransom for many.

The *locus classicus*, however, for the wish to be dissociated from any actual kingship that was connected to the house of David remains Matthew 22:41–46:

> Now while the Pharisees were gathered together, Jesus asked them a question, saying, "What do you think of the Christ [Messiah]? Whose son is he?" They said to him, "The son of David." He said to them, "How is it then that David, inspired by the Spirit, calls him Lord, saying, 'The

Lord said to my Lord, "Sit at my right hand, till I put thy
enemies under thy feet"'? If David thus calls him Lord,
how is he his son?" And no one was able to answer him a
word. (Cf. the earlier version of Mark 12:35–38, which has
in addition: "and the great throng heard him gladly"; Luke
20:41–44)

According to this tradition Jesus dissociated himself publicly from David, who was viewed as a political and na-
tionalistic king. Another example in which kingship is
portrayed in a spiritualistic manner is Matthew 25:31–45:

When the Son of Man comes in his glory, and all the angels
with him, then he will sit on his glorious throne. Before
him will be gathered all the nations....Then the king will
say to those at his right hand, Come, O you blessed of
my Father, inherit the kingdom prepared for you from the
foundation of the world.

It is not accidental that when the woman at Bethany
anointed Jesus, according to Mark 14:3–9, no son of David
was mentioned. Also the passage in Luke 22:24–30 shows
that, according to this particular tradition, kingship is not
connected to David's house and real kings were in fact de-
nounced. In the Gospel of John this trend is very strong. To
give only two examples: In John 6:15 Jesus escaped when
his followers wanted to crown him king. The *locus classicus* in John is 18:33–40: "My kingship is not of this world."
In Jewish literature of the period one can trace a spiritual,
apolitical messiah who is depicted in a somewhat different
light, as for instance, the Son of Man in 1 Enoch 45:1–6 and
46:3–7, 51:2–4, etc. In short, a spiritual messiah was to be
dissociated from politics altogether.

It should be added that when Jesus himself speaks of
the *basileia tou* or the *basileia tōn ouranōn* (in Hebrew *malchut
shamayim*, i.e., the Kingdom of God), he in fact speaks in all
versions *against* the political idea of the kingdom of the son
of David. Without going into the problem of whether Jesus
thought that the *basileia* (kingdom) would be established
in the future or was already there at his present time, one
thing is certain, that Jesus thought neither of the heavenly

kingdom nor of himself in terms of a king with an army, servants, conquests, and territory.[14] He wanted to be some kind of a spiritual king and not a physical and political one. In fact, many of his parables and discourses reveal this. Yet he never draws a concrete plan, as the Hellenistic utopists had done, of the "Kingdom of God." He wanted it to remain as vague as possible (Matthew 13 and 18, 25 mention those who are eligible to enter the Kingdom, but do not describe it).

The concept of the son of David no doubt was dangerous inasmuch as pretenders could always use it freely. Who could really examine the genealogy of one or another pretender to see if he was "genuine"? Thus the more cautious people, and the ones who were anti-kingship in its Herodian form (they existed all the time, as was shown by the circumstances in 63 B.C.E., 4 B.C.E., and 66 C.E.) were opposed to any king who came from a house different from the house of David. One can possibly find this concept in Ps. Philo. In contrast with the figure of Saul in the *Antiquities* of Josephus, in Ps. Philo's Biblical Antiquities there is a strong bias against Saul, who is portrayed as a king who appeared "before his time" and who did not come from David's house. The message of this book is that local figures rather than a false king could help greatly in saving the people of Israel during their clashes with their neighbors in the Land, until the son of David would create a new genuine dynasty. The document was written ca. 70 C.E.[15]

CONCLUSION

Let me now conclude.

1. At the beginning of the first century C.E., after Herod the Great's death, there were attempts by pretenders to revive Herod's dynasty, but these proved to be futile, and I doubt whether they had any kingly ideology behind them as a driving motive.[16] In the 30s, 40s, and 50s of the first century C.E., the only earthly kings who

were around in Palestine were the Jewish successors of
Herod, who were all *but* examples of great earthly kings.
No attempt to revive a Jewish kingdom can be traced until
the move by the Zealots in 66 C.E. to crown their candi-
date Menachem during the start of the great war against
Rome, but this was futile from its outset. Moreover, in the
ideological world of Jesus, the Roman emperor was re-
mote, and therefore he did not constitute an example of an
ugly, earthly king. As already mentioned Jesus despised all
earthly kings, at least according to his later transmitters.

2. Jesus was very much influenced by the spiritual,
heavenly kingdom that, unlike the *Songs of the Sabbath Sacrifice,* was not depicted in architectural lines and had no
clear design.

3. Was Jesus at all close to the "Fourth Philosophy"
group, which according to Josephus said that "only God
can rule" and that every earthly ruler should be removed
by force? One should emphasize that there was a difference
between the rule of God instead of the hateful Romans,
and a Kingdom of God, which was heavenly, amorphous,
and vague. But even if a difference cannot be detected, the
"Fourth Philosophy," which was mentioned by Josephus in
the context of the events of the beginning of the first century (6 C.E.), was not active politically in the sense of using
violence to achieve independence until the years preced-
ing the great war in 66 C.E. Even then, Christian groups
did not participate in the war (Josephus would definitely
have mentioned such a fact). Jesus hence thought in very
vague terms of a heavenly spiritual kingdom and did not
wish to create a new Jewish kingdom in this world, as
Bultmann justifiably said many years ago (therefore John's
comments that the kingdom is not of this world may reflect
early traditions). A real monarchy with army and conquests would have been against the whole raison d'être of
Jesus' ministry.

Let me add that I am also not so sure that the early
Christians were a pacific group like the Pharisees, as Borg
has suggested. The Pharisees, as far as we can learn from

later evidence, were not against a political earthly kingdom, such as the one of David; they were not active in any revolutionary political context from the beginning of the century until 66 C.E. Only then many of them joined the Zealots (Fourth Philosophy group) in the war against Rome. The Pharisees never gave up the idea of a state, whereas Jesus never had an earthly state in mind. Only when the Pharisees realized that the Romans had got the upper hand in the great war (66–70 C.E.) did they decide that Rome was sent by God to punish the Jews, as Jeremiah had once thought, and many of them stopped their armed resistance against Rome.[17]

4. The Gospels did not tone down an aggressive Jesus. Why would they? Josephus did not tone down any hostile Christian aggression against Rome. Such aggression simply did not take place.

NOTES

1. For the history of this issue in modern scholarship see Bammel in his excellent survey in Ernst Bammel and C. F. D. Moule, *Jesus and the Politics of His day* (New York: Cambridge University Press, 1984); and Daniel R. Schwartz, *Studies in the Jewish Background of Christianity,* Wissenschaftliche Untersuchungen zum Neuen Testament 60 (Tübingen: J. C. B. Mohr, 1992). See in general for the question of the historical Jesus John P. Meier, *A Marginal Jew: Rethinking the Historical Jesus* Anchor Bible Reference Library (New York: Doubleday, 1991).

2. For a fresh emphasis on this issue, see Doron Mendels, *The Rise and Fall of Jewish Nationalism: Jewish and Christian Ethnicity in Ancient Palestine* Anchor Bible Reference Library (New York: Doubleday, 1992).

3. For historiography in the New Testament see David E. Aune, *The New Testament in Its Literary Environment,* Library of Early Christianity 8 (Philadelphia: Westminster, 1987).

4. For Josephus in general see P. Villalba i Varneda, *The Historical Method of Flavius Josephus* (Leiden, 1986).

5. See Mendels, *The Rise and Fall,* 35–54, and *passim.*

6. For this issue see Martin Hengel, *The "Hellenization" of*

Judaea in the First Century after Christ (Philadelphia: Trinity Press International, 1989).

7. Marcus J. Borg, *Conflict, Holiness and Politics in the Teachings of Jesus* Studies in the Bible and Early Christianity 5 (New York and Toronto, 1984). Richard A. Horsley, *Jesus and the Spiral of Violence: Popular Jewish Resistance in Roman Palestine* (San Francisco: Harper & Row, 1987).

8. For Euhemerism see John Ferguson, *Utopias of the Classical World* (London: Thames and Hudson, 1975), 102–10.

9. Carol Newsom, *Songs of the Sabbath Sacrifice: A Critical Edition* (Atlanta: Scholars Press, 1985). For kingship at the time see also Martin Hengel and A. M. Schwemer, eds. *Königsherrschaft Gottes und himmlischer Kult* (Tübingen: J. C. B. Mohr [Paul Siebeck], 1991).

10. For this text see Howard Jacobson, *The Exagoge of Ezekiel* (Cambridge: Cambridge University Press, 1983).

11. For the following in more detail see Mendels, *The Rise and Fall*, 209–42.

12. For messianism in general see James H. Charlesworth, *The Messiah: Developments in Earliest Judaism and Christianity*, First Princeton Symposium on Judaism and Christian Origins (Minneapolis: Fortress, 1992).

13. However, during the period under discussion, the Hasmonean dynasty as negatively viewed by some (Psalms of Solomon 17:6 and elsewhere, and the Testament of Moses 5).

14. Recently J. Marcus argued ingeniously that the Jewish War was the setting against which one should read the Gospel of Mark ("The Jewish War and the *Sitz im Leben* of Mark," *Journal of Biblical Literature* 111, no. 3 [1992], 441–62. I saw his article in draft form around March 1991, and we discussed several points. Some of my reservations made then about his important contribution are relevant to the subject of this paper.

a. Marcus's thesis is based on the assumption that the Gospel of Mark was written ca. 70 C.E. (441 and elsewhere). However, it should be emphatically stated that there is no reason to date this document around the year 70 C.E., because the allusions within the document are too vague to be related to specific events. The date of Mark is one of those assumptions that have nourished scholars for decades and are gradually turned into facts.

b. Some of the phrases from Mark 13 as well as 11:17 are too vague to be associated with the Jewish War. Prophecies of this kind were natural within the messianic and eschatological atmosphere in Palestine during the 40s, 50s, and 60s of the first century C.E. Moreover, the expressions "abomination of desolation" (Daniel) and "den of brigands" (Jeremiah) could have been used by Jesus and his successors many years before 70 C.E. to express their disapproval of the Temple, its priesthood, and its service. Also 13:1–2 does not necessarily refer to the *past* destruction of the Temple (again, a common assumption among New Testament scholars).

c. The term *lēstēs* (brigand), used by Mark 11:17, on which Marcus builds a great deal, can already be found in the LXX to Jeremiah 7:11, and thus cannot be taken as an actual allusion to the Zealots of the Jewish War (unless the LXX to Jeremiah was written in reaction to this very war . . .). Be that as it may, *lēstēs* is a very common term used in Hellenistic literature to denote a brigand and is used by Josephus pejoratively to describe the revolutionaries.

d. Marcus argues brilliantly that Mark actually polemicizes against the Zealots, who, he claims, eliminated the universal (i.e., gentile) aspect of the Temple (p. 462 and elsewhere). This contradicts existing evidence because before the war of 67–70 C.E. there is *no* universal or gentile influence in the Temple. The Temple, we know, was abused by Jews, but we never hear of a so-called gentile (i.e., Hellenistic) penetration into it (as in the times of the pre-Maccabean Hellenizers). Mark may have had a universalistic tendency concerning the Temple ("house of prayer for all peoples") in line with Isaiah and Jeremiah, but this is not a point that he could have brought against the Zealots of 66–70, because they were not the ones who changed the status of the Temple in this respect.

e. The argument that Mark "fashioned the 'Davidic' section of his narrative (10:46–12:37) with the claim of figures like Simon and Menachem before his eyes" (p. 459), seems to me somewhat difficult to accept. It is important to note that a "tradition" of entries into Jerusalem existed during the Second Temple period. Judas Maccabeus entered the city and purified the Temple; Herod the great entered Jerusalem as "king of Judaea"; Agrippa I came to Jerusalem on his first entry as king, and went to the Temple. The false prophet from Egypt (Josephus, *Ant.* 20:169–172; *Jewish War* 2:261–63, and perhaps Theudas too, *Ant.* 20:97–98; Acts 5:36) tried to enter the holy city. None of these figures claimed to be of Davidic descent. Thus the description of Jesus' entry, accentuating his being a "son of David," may be seen as polemic *against* all the other entries of people not of Davidic descent into the holy city. In other words, the entry of non-Davidic claimants (including perhaps Menachem and Simon) could have been a good enough reason for Mark to emphasize throughout his story that Jesus *was* of the Davidic house.

Mark's ambivalence (which can also be found in the other synoptics) can hence be explained on the basis of a two-level attitude toward messianism, as is done in my present paper (and see also my *Rise and Fall*). Jesus dissociated himself altogether from earthly kingship in the broader sense of the term and thus from any imminent return of an earthly king of the house of David. This is probably an old tradition going back to the 30s and 40s of the first century C.E.

His followers and "biographers," however, connect him to this line. His followers did this because they thought in "earthly" terms. They needed a concrete symbol of kingship. The evangelists — writing when earthly kingship in Palestine had been passé for many years — fashioned Jesus as a "son of David" in its idealistic form (e.g., in line with Zech. 14; for this issue see Paul Brooks Duff, "The March of the Divine Warrior and the Advent of the Greco-Roman King: Mark's Account of Jesus' Entry into Jerusalem," *Journal of Biblical Literature* 111, no. 1 [1992]: 55–71). It was no longer dangerous to talk about the "son of David" because earthly kingship was not an imminent danger.

15. Doron Mendels, "Pseudo-Philo's Biblical Antiquities, the 'Fourth Philosophy,' and the Political Messianism of the First Century C.E.," in Charlesworth, *The Messiah*, 261–75.

16. Ibid. *passim*.

17. For this concept in Early Judaism, see S. J. D. Cohen, *From the Maccabees to the Mishnah* (Philadelphia: Westminster, 1987).

Conclusion

James H. Charlesworth

The contributors to *Images of Jesus Today* represent the attractive variety of our pluralistic world. One is an ordained minister (Charlesworth), one was converted to Christianity because of his research on the historical Jesus (Borg), one is a historian who has made significant contributions to the elucidation of Christian origins by employing sociological and anthropological models (Horsley), and one is an Israeli who is a recognized expert on Early Judaism and Hellenistic historiography (Mendels). Each has published significantly in the field of Jesus Research.

Together they demonstrate the appropriate methodology for Jesus Research. They make three things pellucidly clear. And they contribute six major insights.

These studies demonstrate the appropriate method in studying the first-century Jewish male named Jesus. Faith — or agnostic — presuppositions must not dictate the answers to our questions; and neither should they limit the range of questions to be raised. The four specialists, along with Professor Weaver, illustrate that Jesus Research has moved away from the theologically rigged methodology that tended to characterize Bultmann (though not all of his students). The present method is free of the myopia of a purely theological approach to Jesus and Christian origins. The previous method sought to elevate the historic and make Jesus meaningful for believers today; but it isolated Jesus, his life and his words, from the Judaism of his day and defined them within the study of the preaching of the earliest "Christians" (the kerygma). Jesus is now portrayed as a first-century Jew whose life and message make eminent sense within what can be known about that time back then and over there.

The five scholars also clarify three things. First, Jesus lived and was influenced by his first-century environment. It is misleading to seek for his uniqueness by focusing on what separates him from his Jewish contemporaries (as was demanded by the criterion of dissimilarity).

Second, our understanding of him is enhanced by the recent acquisition of major primary sources from his day (especially the Dead Sea Scrolls, the Old Testament Pseudepigrapha, and the phenomenal archaeological discoveries revealing the quality of life and religious conviction of Jesus' contemporaries). It is enriched by the application of new methodologies, especially sociologically and anthropologically improved perceptions and models for reconstructing the past.

Third, the Gospels are post-Easter compositions; but they preserve traditions that antedate the crucifixion. These traditions are complex, representing the polemical ambience in which Jesus' first Jewish followers had to struggle for meaning and explanation, especially in Jerusalem and Galilee.

The experts present six major contributions to Jesus Research. First, Jesus Research expands but it is more creative than chaotic. The creative stimulus derives from New Testament specialists leaving the parochialism of Western academia to seek to reconstruct what Jewish life was like in ancient Palestine two thousand years ago.

Second, if scholars are to continue to label Jesus' message as "eschatological," they should explain clearly and fully what is meant by such an adjective. Jesus was not a dreamer about the future. He stressed the importance of the present and reached out to those in need around him, in words couched in simple phrases and pictorial stories and in acts of inclusion that broke down social barriers.

Third, sociological models help us reconstruct Jesus' environment and help us comprehend his life and teaching. They also, especially when employed by Horsley, expose the inappropriateness of some models, especially the portrayal of Jesus and his group in terms of the Cynics, and indicate that Jesus' purpose was shaped by the dynamic conflict between the ruling elites and the so-called peasant majority.

Fourth, no dichotomy between politics and religion is appropriate for Jesus and his culture. It is clear that although Jesus was not a Zealot or political revolutionary, his focus on God's Rule on earth and his intermittent following by mobs would definitely have been seen, and indeed was seen, as a movement with political ramifications.

Fifth, Jesus clearly and certainly challenged boldly and openly his contemporaries' obsessive focus upon purity and the fear of being unclean or unholy, especially as demanded of all by the rich, powerful, and elite Jewish leaders based in Jerusalem.

Sixth, Jesus was a prophet, and it is imperative to explore what he may have inherited from the earlier Israelite prophets (many of whom he quoted).

In conclusion, let me append some personal reflections and reservations. First, Jesus does appear as a radical social prophet (Horsley), but that does not mean he was uninfluenced by the apocalyptic and eschatological fervor of his day. How do we align Jesus' social reform with his apocalyptic and eschatological pronouncements?

Second, Jesus focused on the transformation of the present world ("thy kingdom come on earth"), but that focus does not explain his obvious eschatological and apocalyptic expectations as found, for example, in Mark 9:1. Can Jesus' declaration of the inbreaking of God's Rule (the Kingdom of God) be reduced, as Horsley argues, to a "this-worldly" political metaphor? Does the Qumranic *Songs of the Sabbath Sacrifice*, with its pervasive depictions of God as "King," not help us perceive Jesus' concept of God's kingship? With many — Weiss, Schweitzer, Bultmann, and Sanders — I doubt that Jesus' imminent end-of-the-world eschatology can be easily jettisoned from authentic Jesus tradition (contra Borg, Horsley, and Crossan).

Third, Jesus directed his mission against his society's preoccupation and devotion to purity and patriarchy (Borg and Schüssler Fiorenza are correct), but that does not indicate he was a prophet of wisdom. The Dead Sea Scrolls and Old Testament Pseudepigrapha represent the intellectual world of Jesus' day and caution us against portraying him as merely a this-worldly teacher of wisdom.

Fourth, is Borg right to point to the collapse of a consensus regarding the eschatological Jesus? Is it not more accurate to point to the need for a major revision of what had been meant by this term and to admit that there is less of a consensus here than twenty years ago?

Fifth, it is certain that Jesus did not have an earthly state in mind; but it is not yet clear that he thought only of a heavenly spiritual kingdom. If he chose twelve disciples — and I am convinced that he did — then he was in some ways yet to be discerned attempting to restore Israel in some political sense.

Index of Authors and Subjects